Harcourt
Health and Fitness

Teaching Resources
Grade 5

D1417503

Harcourt
SCHOOL PUBLISHERS

Orlando • Austin • New York • San Diego • Toronto • London

Visit *The Learning Site!*
www.harcourtschool.com

Contents

Health Resources

School–Home Connection Letters

Writing Models

Contents (Continued)

Organizers

Health and Safety Handbook **75**

Activity Book Answer Key **137**

Teaching Resources Answer Key **141**

Resources for the Coordinated School Health Program

This directory lists agencies that provide support for the eight different aspects of the Coordinated School Health Program and will aid you in your classroom planning and teaching activities.
While every effort has been made to provide complete and accurate website addresses, the nature of the World Wide Web makes it impossible to follow every link on every site to ensure reliable and up-to-date information. Please use your own discretion about the suitability of the material found on a site, and preview any site to which you refer your students.

Advocates for Youth
1025 Vermont Ave., NW, Suite 210
Washington, DC 20005
Phone: (202) 347-5700
Fax: (202) 347-2263
http://www.advocatesforyouth.org

American Academy of Child & Adolescent Psychiatry
3615 Wisconsin Ave., NW
Washington, DC 20016-3007
Phone: (202) 966-7300
Fax: (202) 966-2891
http://www.aacap.org

American Academy of Pediatrics
141 Northwest Point Blvd.
Elk Grove Village, IL 60007
Phone: (847) 434-4000
Fax: (847) 434-8000
http://www.aap.org

American Association for Active Lifestyles & Fitness
1900 Association Dr.
Reston, VA 22091
Phone: (800) 213-7193
Fax: (703) 476-9527
http://www.aahperd.org/aaalf/aaalfmain.html

American Association for Health Education
1900 Association Dr.
Reston, VA 22091
Phone: (703) 476-3437
Fax: (703) 476-6638
http://www.aahperd.org/aahe/aahemain.html

American Association of School Administrators
1801 N. Moore St.
Arlington, VA 22209
Phone: (703) 528-0700
Fax: (703) 841-1543
http://www.aasa.org

American Cancer Society
1599 Clifton Rd., NE
Atlanta, GA 30329
Phone: (800) 227-2345
Fax: (404) 248-1780
http://www.cancer.org

American College of Sports Medicine
401 W. Michigan St.
Indianapolis, IN 46202-3233
Phone: (317) 637-9200
Fax: (317) 634-7817
http://www.acsm.org

American Dietetic Association
216 W. Jackson Blvd., Suite 800
Chicago, IL 60606
Phone: (312) 899-0040
Fax: (312) 899-1758
http://www.eatright.org

American Federation of Teachers
555 New Jersey Ave., NW
Washington, DC 20001
Phone: (202) 879-4490
Fax: (202) 393-8648
http://www.aft.org

American Medical Association
514 N. State St.
Chicago, IL 60610
Phone: (312) 464-5000
Fax: (312) 464-5842
http://www.ama-assn.org

American Nurses Association
600 Maryland Ave., SW
Suite 100 West
Washington, DC 20024
Phone: (800) 274-4262
Fax: (202) 651-7001
http://www.ana.org

American Psychological Association
750 First St., NE
Washington, DC 20002
Phone: (800) 374-2721
Fax: (202) 336-5962
http://www.apa.org

American Public Health Association
800 I St., NW
Washington, DC 20001-3710
Phone: (202) 777-2742
Fax: (202) 777-2534
http://www.apha.org

American Public Human Services Association
810 First St., NE, Suite 500
Washington, DC 20002
Phone: (202) 682-0100
Fax: (202) 289-6555
http://www.aphsa.org

American Red Cross
8111 Gatehouse Rd.
Jefferson Park
Falls Church, VA 22042
Phone: (703) 206-7180
Fax: (703) 206-7673
http://www.redcross.org

American School Counselor Association
801 N. Fairfax St., Suite 310
Alexandria, VA 22314
Phone: (703) 683-2722
Fax: (703) 683-1619
http://www.schoolcounselor.org

American School Food Service Association
700 South Washington St., Suite 300
Alexandria, VA 22314
Phone: (703) 739-3900
Fax: (703) 739-3915
http://www.asfsa.org

American School Health Association
PO Box 708
Kent, OH 44240
Phone: (330) 678-1601
Fax: (330) 678-4526
http://www.ashaweb.org

Association for Supervision & Curriculum Development
1703 North Beauregard St.
Alexandria, VA 22311-1714
Phone: (703) 578-9600
Fax: (703) 575-5400
http://www.ascd.org

Association of Maternal & Child Health Programs
1220 19 St., NW, Suite 801
Washington, DC 20036
Phone: (202) 775-0436
Fax: (202) 775-0061
http://www.amchp.org

Association of State & Territorial Chronic Disease Program Directors
111 Park Place
Falls Church, VA 22046-4513
Phone: (703) 538-1798
Fax: (703) 241-5603
http://www.astcdpd.org

Association of State & Territorial Dental Directors
322 Cannondale Rd.
Jefferson City, MO 65109
Phone: (573) 636-0453
Fax: (573) 636-0454
http://www.astdd.org

Association of State & Territorial Directors of Health Promotion and Public Health Education
750 First St., NE, Suite 1050
Washington, DC 20002
Phone: (202) 312-6460
Fax: (202) 336-6012
http://www.astdhpphe.org

Association of State & Territorial Health Officials
1275 K St., NW, Suite 800
Washington, DC 20005
Phone: (202) 371-9090
Fax: (202) 371-9797
http://www.astho.org

Association of State & Territorial Public Health Nutrition Directors
1015 15 St., NW, Suite 800
Washington, DC 20005
Phone: (202) 408-1257
Fax: (202) 408-1259
http://www.astphnd.org

California Department of Education
Safe and Healthy Kids Program Office
1430 N. Street, Suite 6408
Sacramento, CA 95814
Phone: (916) 319-0920
Fax: (916) 319-0218
http://www.cde.ca.gov/healthykids

California Healthy Kids Resource Center
313 W. Winton Ave., Room 180
Hayward, CA 94544
Phone: (510) 670-4581
Fax: (510) 670-4582
http://www.hkresources.org

Center for School Mental Health Assistance
University of Maryland-Baltimore,
Department of Psychiatry
680 W. Lexington St., 10th Floor
Baltimore, MD 21201-1570
Phone: (410) 706-0980
Fax: (410) 706-0984
http://www.csmha.umaryland.edu/
csmha2001/main.php3

Centers for Disease Control and Prevention (CDC)
1600 Clifton Rd., NE
Atlanta, GA 30333
Phone: (404) 639-3311
http://www.CDC.gov

Communities in Schools, Inc.
227 S. Washington St., Suite 210
Alexandria, VA 22314
Phone: (703) 519-8999
Fax: (703) 519-7213
http://www.clsnet.org

The Council for Exceptional Children
1110 N. Glebe Rd., Suite 300
Arlington, VA 22201-5704
Phone: (703) 620-3660
Fax: (703) 264-9494
http://www.cec.sped.org

Council of Chief State School Officers
One Massachusetts Ave., NW
Suite 700
Washington, DC 20001
Phone: (202) 408-5505
Fax: (202) 408-8072
http://www.ccsso.org

Council of the Great City Schools
1301 Pennsylvania Ave., NW
Suite 702
Washington, DC 20004
Phone: (202) 393-2427
Fax: (202) 393-2400
http://www.cgcs.org

Employee Assistance Professionals Association
2102 Wilson Blvd., Suite 500
Arlington, VA 22201
Phone: (703) 387-1000
Fax: (703) 522-4585
http://www.eap-association.org

Food Research and Action Center
1875 Connecticut Ave., NW,
Suite 540
Washington, DC 20009
Phone: (202) 986-2200
Fax: (202) 986-2525
http://www.frac.org

National Alliance for the Mentally Ill
Colonial Place Three
2107 Wilson Blvd., Suite 300
Arlington, VA 22201
Phone: (703) 524-7600
Fax: (703) 524-9094
http://www.nami.org

National Alliance of Pupil Services Organizations
7700 Willowbrook Rd.
Fairfax Station, VA 22039
Phone: (703) 250-3414
Fax: (703) 250-6324
https://www.socialworkers.org/

National Assembly on School-Based Health Care
666 11th St., NW, Suite 735
Washington, DC 20001
Phone: (888) 286-8727
Fax: (202) 638-5879
http://www.nasbhc.org

National Association for Sport and Physical Education
1900 Association Dr.
Reston, VA 20191-1599
Phone: (703) 476-3410
Fax: (703) 476-8316
http://www.aahperd.org/naspe/naspemain.html

National Association of Community Health Centers
1330 New Hampshire Ave., NW
Suite 122
Washington, DC 20036
Phone: (202) 659-8008
Fax: (202) 659-8519
http://www.nachc.org

National Association of County & City Health Officials
1100 17th St., NW, 2nd Floor
Washington, DC 20036
Phone: (202) 783-5550
Fax: (202) 783-1583
http://www.naccho.org

National Association of Elementary School Principals
1615 Duke St.
Alexandria, VA 22314
Phone: (703) 684-3345
Fax: (703) 518-6281
http://www.naesp.org

National Association of Health & Fitness
201 S. Capitol Ave., Suite 560
Indianapolis, IN 46225
Phone: (317) 237-5630
Fax: (317) 237-5632
http://www.physicalfitness.org

National Association of Leadership for Student Assistance Programs
PO Box 335
Bedminster, PA 18910
Phone: (215) 795-2119
Fax: (215) 795-0822

National Association of School Nurses
PO Box 1300
Scarborough, ME 04074-1300
Phone: (207) 883-2117
Fax: (207) 883-2683
http://www.nasn.org

National Association of School Psychologists
4340 East West Hwy., Suite 402
Bethesda, MD 20814
Phone: (301) 657-0270
Fax: (301) 657-0275
http://www.nasponline.org

National Association of Social Workers
750 First St., NE, Suite 700
Washington, DC 20002-4241
Phone: (202) 408-8600
Fax: (202) 336-8310
http://www.naswdc.org

National Association of State Boards of Education
277 S. Washington St., Suite 100
Alexandria, VA 22314
Phone: (703) 684-4000
Fax: (703) 836-2313
http://www.nasbe.org

National Association of State NET Program Coordinators
200 W. Baltimore St.
Baltimore, MD 21201
Phone: (410) 767-0222
Fax: (410) 333-2635

National Coalition for Parent Involvement in Education
3929 Old Lee Hwy., Suite 91-A
Fairfax, VA 22030-2401
Phone: (703) 359-8973
Fax: (703) 359-0972
http://www.ncpie.org

National Coalition of Chapter 1 and Title 1 Parents
Edmonds Schools Building
9th and D Sts., NE, Room 201
Washington, DC 20002
Phone: (202) 547-9286
Fax: (202) 547-2813
http://www.nctic1p.org/

National Conference of State Legislatures
1560 Broadway, Suite 700
Denver, CO 80202
Phone: (303) 830-2200
Fax: (303) 863-8003
http://www.ncsl.org

National Council of Churches
475 Riverside Dr.
New York, NY 10115
Phone: (212) 870-2297
Fax: (212) 870-2030
http://www.nccusa.org

National Council of LaRaza
1111 19th St., NW, Suite 1000
Washington, DC 20036
Phone: (202) 785-1670
Fax: (202) 776-1792
http://www.nclr.org

National Education Association
1201 16th St., NW
Washington, DC 20036
Phone: (202) 883-4000
Fax: (202) 822-7775
http://www.nea.org

National Environmental Health Association
720 South Colorado Blvd., Suite 970-S
Denver, CO 80246
Phone: (303) 756-9090
Fax: (303) 691-9490
http://www.neha.org

National Federation of State High School Associations
PO Box 690
Indianapolis, IN 46206
Phone: (317) 972-6900
Fax: (317) 822-5700
http://www.nfhs.org

National Middle School Association
4151 Executive Parkway, Suite 300
Westerville, OH 43081
Phone: (800) 528-6672
Fax: (614) 895-4750
http://www.nmsa.org

National Network for Youth
1319 F St., NW, Suite 401
Washington, DC 20004
Phone: (202) 783-7949
Fax: (202) 783-7955
http://www.nn4youth.org

National Peer Helpers Association
PO Box 2684
Greenville, NC 27834
Phone: (877) 314-7337
Fax: (919) 522-3959
http://www.peerhelping.org

The National PTA
330 N. Wabash Ave., Suite 2100
Chicago, IL 60611-3690
Phone: (312) 670-6782
Fax: (312) 670-6783
http://www.pta.org

National Safety Council
1121 Spring Lake Dr.
Itasca, IL 60143-3201
Phone: (630) 285-1121
Fax: (630) 285-1315
http://www.nsc.org

National School Boards Association
1680 Duke St.
Alexandria, VA 22314
Phone: (703) 838-6722
Fax: (703) 683-7590
http://www.nsba.org

National Urban League
120 Wall St., 8th Floor
New York, NY 10005
Phone: (212) 558-5300
Fax: (212) 344-5332
http://www.nul.org

National Wellness Association
PO Box 827
Stevens Point, WI 54481-0827
Phone: (715) 342-2969
Fax: (715) 342-2979
http://www.nationalwellness.org

President's Council for Physical Fitness and Sports
Hubert H. Humphrey Building
200 Independence Ave., SW, Room 738H
Washington, DC 20201
Phone: (202) 690-9000
Fax: (202) 690-5211
http://www.fitness.gov

Public Education Network
601 13th St., NW, Suite 900 North
Washington, DC 20005
Phone: (202) 628-7460
Fax: (202) 628-1893
http://www.publiceducation.org

Public Risk Management Association
1815 N. Fort Meyer Dr., Suite 102
Arlington, VA 22209
Phone: (703) 528-7701
Fax: (703) 528-7966
http://www.primacentral.org

Society for Adolescent Medicine
1916 Copper Oaks Circle
Blue Springs, MO 64015
Phone: (816) 224-8010
Fax: (816) 224-8009
http://www.adolescenthealth.org

Society for Nutrition Education
1001 Connecticut Ave., NW, Suite 528
Washington, DC 20036-5528
Phone: (202) 452-8534
Fax: (202) 452-8536
http://www.sne.org

Society for Public Health Education, Inc.
750 First St., NE, Suite 910
Washington, DC 20002-4242
Phone: (202) 408-9804
Fax: (202) 408-9815
http://www.sophe.org

Society of State Directors of Health, Physical Education, and Recreation
1900 Association Dr.
Reston, VA 21091-1599
Phone: (703) 476-3402
Fax: (703) 476-9527
http://www.thesociety.org

State Directors of Child Nutrition
C/O AFSA
700 S. Washington St., Suite 300
Alexandria, VA 22314
Phone: (703) 739-3900
Fax: (703) 739-3915
http://www.asfsa.org

Wellness Councils of America
9802 Nicholas St., Suite 315
Omaha, NE 68114
Phone: (402) 827-3590
Fax: (402) 827-3594
http://www.welcoa.org

Diseases and Disorders: Background, Symptoms, and Classroom Implications

The following information about various communicable and noncommunicable diseases and disorders is provided for your reference. Background information, signs/symptoms, and school or classroom implications are given for each disease. Consult your school nurse or another medical authority if you have any questions or concerns about the health of your students.

Communicable Diseases and Disorders	Noncommunicable Diseases and Disorders
Chicken Pox (Varicella)	Anorexia Nervosa
Colds	Anthrax
Conjunctivitis (Pinkeye)	Appendicitis
Fifth Disease	Asthma
Hepatitis (Viral)	Bronchitis (Asthmatic or Allergic)
Human Immunodeficiency Virus (HIV) Infection and Acquired Immunodeficiency Syndrome (AIDS)	Cerebral Palsy (CP)
	Diabetes
	Down Syndrome
Impetigo	Epilepsy (Seizure Disorder)
Influenza	Hearing Loss
Measles (Rubella, or German Measles)	Heart Disorders
	Hemophilia (Bleeding Disorder)
Measles (Rubeola)	Leukemia
Infectious Mononucleosis (Mono)	Lyme Disease
Mumps	Muscular Dystrophy
Pediculosis (Lice)	Peptic Ulcer
Ringworm (Tinea)	Reye's Syndrome
Scabies	Rheumatic Fever
Smallpox	Rheumatoid Arthritis
Staphylococcal Infections (Staph)	Scoliosis
Strep Throat	Sickle-Cell Anemia
Sudden Acute Respiratory Syndrome (SARS)	Sty
	Tendonitis
Tonsillitis	Tetanus (Lockjaw)
Tuberculosis (TB)	Vision Disorders
	West Nile Virus

Communicable Diseases and Disorders

Infectious conditions, whether communicable among humans or noncommunicable, are receiving more medical and media attention. While much conversation is about agents that might be adapted to hurt or threaten groups, e.g., inhalation anthrax or smallpox, there is much more occurring with "emerging" and re-emerging infections. Several factors are involved: global work that exposes people to new infectious agents; intercontinental travel of people and transportation of animals that harbor infection or objects and insects that can transmit disease (vectors); population increases and crowding; public health and laboratory tests that can identify new organisms and give more specific reasons for illnesses; disrupted habitats (irrigation, deforestation) that allow organisms to jump to another species of animal; contaminated water as breeding ground for organisms; food preparation and distribution across the world; lagging vaccination rates; unrecognized "old" contagious conditions like whooping cough and tuberculosis; microbe resistance to drugs and pesticides; and fewer public health resources for malaria.

Chicken Pox (Varicella)

Background: Chicken pox (varicella) is caused by the varicella zoster virus. This virus can become dormant in nerve cells and later re-activate as shingles. Chicken pox is a relatively mild disease in children without other chronic conditions. However, Reye's syndrome, which can have serious results, is often preceded by salicylate (aspirin) use in viral illnesses such as chicken pox (see "Reye's syndrome" under "Noncommunicable Diseases and Disorders"). A vaccine is available for children between ages 12 and 18 months or older children who have not had varicella.

Symptoms: mild headache and moderate fever, a rash progressing to itching fluid-filled blisters, which then scab and crust over

Classroom Implications: Chicken pox is highly contagious and is spread by direct contact with blister fluid and through nasal discharge. Students may return to school when all the blisters have crusted over. Some may have complications such as pneumonia or secondary skin infection which delay their return.

Colds

Background: Colds are caused by viruses. More than a hundred such viruses have been found to produce the inflammatory reactions associated with colds. Therefore, colds can occur as many as four or five times a year. The key factor is exposure to an infected person. Being chilled does not cause a cold but may lower resistance to developing the disease after exposure.

Symptoms: a tickling sensation in the nose and throat, bouts of sneezing, watery nasal discharge, dulled senses of taste and smell, body aches, a cough, slight fever

Classroom Implications: Because cold and influenza viruses are highly infectious, a child with a "blossoming" cold (fever, cough, sneezes) should probably not be in school. However, many students attend school while recovering. Reinforcing hygiene with students, such as washing the hands regularly and covering the mouth with disposable tissue when coughing or sneezing, may limit the spread. Remember that a student with a fever/cold does not function at his or her best.

Diseases and Disorders

Conjunctivitis (Pinkeye)

Background: Conjunctivitis can be caused by viruses, bacteria, or allergies. Conjunctivitis is an inflammation of the membrane that covers the cornea or sclera (the white of the eye). Usually the condition is self-limiting. Viral pinkeye is contagious but there is no anti-viral treatment.

Symptoms: pink or red sclera, possibly discharge or crust on the eyelids, itching

Classroom Implications: Viral conjunctivitis is more contagious than bacterial. A student suspected of having pinkeye should be referred to the school nurse. Students should keep their hands clean, not share eye makeup (older girls), and not share face cloths with anyone who has pinkeye.

Fifth Disease

Background: Fifth disease is a mild illness caused by a virus (human parvovirus B19) usually during elementary school age years. If a woman gets the disease during pregnancy, it can infect the unborn child and, in rare cases, cause complications or death to the fetus. The virus is most likely spread by direct contact with saliva or nasal discharge.

Symptoms: begins with signs of a cold but develops a light red "lacy" rash that tends to come and go on the face, the trunk, and the arms and legs. In adults, joint swelling and pain can also occur.

Classroom Implications: Fifth disease is contagious before the rash appears, so it is often not diagnosed until children are no longer contagious. Children are not usually out of school unless running a fever. A pregnant teacher should discuss exposure with her doctor.

Hepatitis (Viral)

Background: Hepatitis is inflammation of the liver. Different viruses are known to cause some cases of viral hepatitis. They are named hepatitis A, B, C, D, and E viruses. All of them cause short-term, viral hepatitis. Hepatitis B, C, and D viruses can also cause chronic hepatitis, in which the infection is sometimes lifelong. Hepatitis A and E are spread through fecal contamination of water and food. Hepatitis B is spread through blood and certain body secretions, such as by sexual activity, blood exposure during childbirth, and the sharing of used needles for tattoos or drug use. Hepatitis C, the most common form, is spread by infected blood, less often by sexual activity or childbirth. Vaccines are available for hepatitis A and hepatitis B. Hepatitis D can occur in persons with hepatitis B.

Symptoms: nausea, vomiting, fever, loss of appetite during the early phase; jaundice, characterized by dark urine and light-color stools (feces) followed by yellowing of the body surfaces and the whites of the eyes (after three to ten days). Young children may have no signs of illness.

Classroom Implications: Though viral hepatitis resolves within weeks, it is a serious illness. General school exposure does not merit immune globulin. If more than one student in a class contracts hepatitis A, it may be prudent to ask about immune globulin for close contacts in the class. These injections provide some short-term protection against the virus. Good personal hygiene, such as washing hands carefully after changing diapers or helping younger children in the toilet, prevents the spread of the disease and should be emphasized. A student who misses school because of hepatitis will likely require home teaching until recovery is complete.

Human Immunodeficiency Virus (HIV) Infection and Acquired Immunodeficiency Syndrome (AIDS)

Background: HIV is the virus that causes AIDS. Most people with HIV infection develop AIDS.

The virus attacks the body's immune system, and infected people become susceptible to a variety of diseases that are usually not serious threats to people with normal immune systems. The AIDS diagnosis is determined by the presence of these infections and by blood tests. HIV is transmitted through contact with specific body fluids, including blood, semen, and vaginal secretions. It is not spread through the air, water, food, eating utensils, tears, sweat, or skin-to-skin contact. Early diagnosis and new drug treatments may interfere with the virus replication and reduce the risk of developing life-threatening infections.

Symptoms: nonspecific symptoms such as swollen lymph glands, loss of appetite, chronic diarrhea, weight loss, fever and fatigue; secondary viral and bacterial infections and cancers such as Kaposi's sarcoma

Classroom Implications: Most people can avoid exposure to HIV by avoiding risky behaviors such as unprotected sex and the sharing of needles. District health services policy should include guidelines to prevent exposure to body secretions, e.g., access to latex or vinyl gloves when assisting in first aid or direct health care.

Impetigo

Background: Impetigo is a skin infection seen mostly in children. It is usually caused by strains of streptococcal or staphylococcal bacteria. The infection usually appears on the fingers or face and is treated with antibiotics.

Symptoms: small blisters with pus; itchy, weeping sores that develop yellow, honey-colored crusts

Classroom Implications: Impetigo may be spread by direct contact. Students who have unexplained sores should be referred to the school nurse. Untreated lesions may cause scarring. Secondary infections in other parts of the body are possible. Students should be reminded to wash their hands and keep their fingernails clean. Sores should be lightly covered while under treatment to limit scratching or exposure to others.

Influenza

Background: The most frequent cause is the influenza A virus. It is spread by person-to-person contact and by droplets that become airborne because of coughing, sneezing, or talking. Major epidemics occur about every three years and affect persons of all ages. Influenza is most prevalent in school children. The very young, the aged, and persons with a chronic condition such as asthma, sickle-cell anemia, or diabetes are at the greatest risk of developing complications. Each year a vaccine is formulated to protect against the flu viruses expected to circulate the following winter. Those at greatest risk of complications from the virus should be among the first to receive the vaccine.

Symptoms: chills, fever, body aches and pains, headache, sore throat, cough, fatigue

Classroom Implications: Influenza is a self-limiting disease, with acute illness lasting for two to three days. Weakness and fatigue may persist for several days or occasionally for weeks. When a student returns to class after a bout with influenza, he or she may temporarily lack the ability to concentrate.

Measles (Rubella, or German Measles)

Background: Rubella is caused by a virus and is spread through personal contact and through airborne droplets. Rubella is milder and less contagious than rubeola, another type of measles. However, a pregnant woman who contracts rubella in early pregnancy risks serious injury to the fetus.

Symptoms: a rash that eventually covers the body, lasting about three days; mild fever; tenderness and swelling of the lymph nodes at the back of the neck

Classroom Implications: Prevention of rubella is a health priority because of the high risk during pregnancy. Children may be vaccinated between 12 and 15 months of age with a combination measles-mumps-rubella (MMR) vaccine and given a booster after age 4 years.

Measles (Rubeola)

Background: Rubeola is caused by a virus that is spread by nose, throat, and mouth droplets. It is most contagious two to four days before the rash begins and during the acute phase. Children should be vaccinated against rubeola. The recommended age for inoculation is between 12 and 15 months with a booster after age 4 years or by age 12 years if not done previously. The combined measles-mumps-rubella (MMR) vaccine is used.

Symptoms: high fever followed by hacking cough, sneezing, runny nose, redness of the eyes, sensitivity to light, a rash beginning at the face and moving down

Classroom Implications: About 20 percent of measles cases develop complications such as ear infections, pneumonia, or even encephalitis with lasting effects. All rubeola cases should be reported to the health authorities.

Infectious Mononucleosis (Mono)

Background: Infectious mononucleosis is caused by the Epstein-Barr virus, which is one of the herpes group of viruses. Mono is often called the "kissing disease," because it is spread by close contact with infected saliva. Mono is not very contagious. It may be positively diagnosed by a blood test.

Symptoms: fatigue, headache, chills, followed by high fever, sore throat, swelling of the lymph nodes. Enlargement of the spleen occurs in some.

Classroom Implications: Infection with the Epstein-Barr virus occurs commonly in children but often goes unrecognized, as it resembles a bad cold. Infectious mononucleosis, as described above, is predominantly more serious for adolescents and young adults. Symptoms can last weeks, and a variety of complications can occur. Many students with mono are out of school a long time and may be easily fatigued when allowed to return, which should be taken into consideration.

Mumps

Background: Mumps is caused by a virus that is spread by droplet infection or by materials that have been in contact with infected saliva. The virus predominantly affects the parotid salivary glands, which are located in the cheek area, in front of the ears. When infected, these glands swell, giving the person a chipmunk-like appearance. Occasionally, the salivary glands under the tongue become involved, and the neck area may swell.

Symptoms: chills, headache, loss of appetite, fever, pain when chewing or swallowing

Classroom Implications: Children may be vaccinated against mumps between ages 12 and 15 months with a booster after age 4 years (before entering school). The vaccine is usually given in a combined form with the measles and rubella vaccines. All mumps cases should be reported to the proper health authorities.

Pediculosis (Lice)

Background: Lice are small parasitic insects. Three types of lice are known to live on a human host. Crab lice *(Phthirus pubis)* are usually transmitted by very close contact, such as during sex or sharing a bed or towel. Body lice *(Pediculus humanus corporis)* are uncommon under good hygienic conditions. Head lice *(Pediculus humanus capitis)* are transmitted by personal contact: by contact with an infested person (contact is common during play at school and at home at slumber parties, during sports activities, at camp, or on a playground); by wearing infested clothing, such as hats, scarves, coats, sports helmets, or hair ribbons; by using infested combs, brushes, or towels; by lying on a bed, couch, pillow, carpet, or stuffed animal that has recently been in contact with an infested person.

Head lice invade the scalp but can also move to the eyebrows, eyelashes, and other facial hair. The lice lay eggs, called nits, which are grayish white and can be seen adhering to the hair shafts. The nits mature in three to fourteen days.

Symptoms: itching, white nits (eggs) that tightly adhere to the hair shafts

Classroom Implications: Teachers should reinforce prevention habits and limit "head-to-head" group work as well as observe for possible signs, e.g., scratching. If a student in class has lice, other students should be discreetly checked with a hand lens by a person trained to identify lice and nits. The lice can be killed with specially medicated shampoo or creams. Parents/caretakers should be advised to remove the nits to prevent re-infestation. Students should be welcomed back in the classroom following effective treatment.

Ringworm (Tinea)

Background: Ringworm is an infection caused by any of a number of fungi that invade only the dead tissue (keratin) of skin, hair or nails. Infection by a certain fungus can produce raised rings on the skin (hence the name *ringworm*). However, other fungi cause different signs. The various fungi attack specific areas of the body.

Symptoms: slowly spreading, scaly, ring-shaped spots on the skin (ringworm of the body, *tinea corporis*); scaling lesions between the toes ("athlete's foot," *tinea pedis*); thickened, lusterless nails with a darkened appearance (ringworm of the nails, *tinea unguium*); small, scaly lesions on the scalp and semibald, grayish patches with broken, lusterless hairs (ringworm of the scalp, *tinea capitis*)

Classroom Implications: The most common types of ringworm are "athlete's foot" and ringworm of the scalp. Athlete's foot is often spread at swimming pools and in showers, locker rooms, and other such wet facilities. Ringworm of the scalp mainly affects children. If this condition is suspected, a student should immediately be referred to the school nurse. Scalp ringworm requires oral prescribed medication to penetrate the hair follicles.

Scabies

Background: Scabies is an infectious parasitic skin infection caused by the itch mite *(Sarcoptes scabiei)*. Pregnant female mites tunnel into the skin and deposit their eggs. The larvae hatch after a few days and group around the hair follicles. Itching is due to hypersensitivity to the parasites' waste products. Scabies is transmitted through prolonged, not casual, skin-to-skin contact, often infecting entire households. It can be spread through shared clothing or bedding.

Symptoms: intense itching; burrows (fine, wavy, dark lines with small pimple-like lesions at the open ends) occurring commonly between the fingers; burrows also occurring on the insides of the wrists and in skin folds on the abdomen and elbows

Classroom Implications: Suspected scabies needs to be referred to health professionals and treated immediately. Prescribed lotions are necessary and the student may also have medication to relieve itching, which can last a month after treatment while dead skin and mites are shed.

Smallpox

Background: Smallpox is a highly contagious disease that was eliminated in the world in 1977. Vaccination was no longer indicated and the vaccine can have serious side effects. There is some concern that the smallpox virus could be used as a weapon of bioterrorism. There is a smallpox preparedness program to protect Americans against smallpox as a biological weapon. This program includes training teams to respond to a smallpox attack. Healthcare and public health workers are being vaccinated in order to care for and vaccinate others in the event of an outbreak. There is enough smallpox vaccine to vaccinate everyone who would need it.

Symptoms: The incubation period for smallpox is from 7 to 17 days following contact with the virus. Symptoms include high fever, fatigue, headache, and backache. A rash follows in 2 to 3 days. The rash begins as a flat red spot that becomes filled with pus and then begins to crust early in the second week. Scabs form and then fall off after 3 to 4 weeks.

Classroom Implications: Smallpox is spread from person to person by infected droplets of saliva. Persons are most contagious during the first week of illness but may be contagious during the entire period of illness. There is no cure for smallpox, but if the vaccine is given within 4 days of exposure to the virus, it can lessen the severity of the illness or even prevent it.

Staphylococcal Infections (Staph)

Background: Staphylococcal bacteria are commonly found on the skin of healthy people. Those who are hospitalized or work in hospitals have a slightly higher incidence of penicillin-resistant strains. Staph food poisoning is caused by the toxin produced by the staphylococci in contaminated food.

Symptoms: General: fever, headache; Skin: boils, abscesses, skin lesions with pus (impetigo); Food: vomiting

Classroom Implications: All staph infections should be treated promptly by a health professional. Suspect food poisoning when a number of people develop vomiting within hours of eating a food in common, often involving improperly prepared or stored products. Report names, symptoms and food(s) eaten, because staph is just one of the possible culprits.

Strep Throat

Background: Strep throat is caused by one form of streptococcal bacterium. A throat culture can confirm the presence of streptococcal bacteria.

Symptoms: sudden fever and headache, sore, beefy-red throat, nausea or vomiting, swollen neck "glands"; inflamed tonsils with thin white patches on tonsils. Cases that include a rash that is due to a toxin produced by the strep bacteria are called scarletina or scarlet fever.

Classroom Implications: Complications of strep throat can be life-threatening. Rheumatic fever with joint or heart disease or a kidney complication may develop in a small percentage of cases. Therefore, it is very important that students who show symptoms of the disease be evaluated. Any student with fever and sore throat without a cough, laryngitis, or stuffy nose should be suspect.

Sudden Acute Respiratory Syndrome (SARS)

Background: This unusual pneumonia is believed to be caused by a virus in the coronavirus family that exists in wild animals used for food in China. With laboratory advances, the cause of SARS was determined within three months of the early cases—great progress compared to the four years it took to identify HIV.

Symptoms: After 2 to 7 (up to 10) days from exposure, an ill person has fever (over 100°), headache, muscle aches, dry cough, and difficulty breathing.

Classroom Implications: With travel restrictions, young students are unlikely to be exposed. Travelers, family, or health workers exposed to infected persons must stay home for a 10-day "health watch" to monitor for symptoms. Infection control includes standard precautions (hand washing) and air precautions (surgical mask for the patient, air filtration in hospitals) with patients with symptoms and exposure. This is a topic that can be used to encourage students to apply the "disease detective" work of epidemiology to an array of health conditions.

Tonsillitis

Background: Tonsillitis is an acute inflammation of the tonsils, often caused by viruses or common bacteria.

Symptoms: sore throat and pain, especially upon swallowing; fever, headache, vomiting, white patches on the tonsils

Classroom Implications: Repeated tonsillitis may cause frequent absences pending medical evaluation. When students return to school after tonsillectomies, there are usually few restrictions on their activity.

Tuberculosis (TB)

Background: Tuberculosis is an acute or chronic disease caused by a rod-shaped bacterium. TB is primarily a pulmonary disease but can strike other organs and tissues, such as bones. Infection usually occurs after exposure from inhaling infectious droplets. The bacteria settle in the lower or middle section of the lungs and multiply. The body's immune system then fights the disease, producing antibodies against it. Infection may continue to be contained without disease developing. The bacteria may reactivate in persons with lowered resistance due to other chronic conditions. TB exposure is detected by the tuberculin skin test (PPD), and disease is determined by lab tests and a chest X–ray.

Symptoms: fever, body aches, chronic cough that expels sputum

Classroom Implications: In the United States TB has reemerged as a serious public health problem, affecting low income groups that live in close quarters and persons who do not get tested or who do not complete treatment. Drug-resistant cases of TB have also increased dramatically because of incomplete treatment. TB is primarily an airborne disease. Children do not cough deeply enough to spread TB bacteria if they have an infection. Public health officials hire staff to ensure that some infected persons complete their antibiotic treatment to avoid more drug-resistance and spread to others.

Noncommunicable Diseases and Disorders

Anorexia Nervosa

Background: Anorexia nervosa is a psychological condition, an eating disorder that is usually most common among adolescent girls. The disease is characterized by a distorted concept of body image and involves extreme weight loss. Many people with the disorder look emaciated but are convinced they are overweight. Bulimia nervosa is a variant of anorexia nervosa. It is characterized by eating binges followed by purges. Purging may involve vomiting, abusing laxatives or diuretics, taking enemas, exercising obsessively, or a combination of these. As body fat decreases, the menstrual cycle is interrupted.

Symptoms: rapid weight loss, change in eating habits, obsession with exercise to lose weight, increased use of laxatives, depressed mental state, cessation of menstruation, sores around the mouth and dental disease from forced vomiting

Classroom Implications: Eating disorders such as anorexia nervosa and bulimia nervosa may occur in varying severity. They are more successfully treated when diagnosed early. Many cases have been discovered by teachers who have made appropriate referrals. Students with eating disorders need the emotional support of their teachers. Efforts to enhance realistic body image and self-concept in the classroom contribute toward treatment goals.

Anthrax

Background: Anthrax is a noncommunicable infectious disease usually found in cloven-hoofed animals. It can also infect humans. Anthrax infection takes one of three possible forms. They are inhalation, cutaneous, and gastrointestinal. Inhalation anthrax involves inhaling *Bacillus anthracis*. This is the most serious form of infection. Cutaneous, or skin infection, involves transmission through a cut or rash on the skin. This is the least serious form of infection but has been around for centuries. Gastrointestinal infection occurs when infected meat is ingested. Between January 1955 and December 1999, there were 236 reported cases of anthrax in the United States. Most of those cases were cutaneous and occurred among persons who worked with contaminated animal products. Anthrax has been used as an agent of bioterrorism within the United States. A vaccine is available for the prevention of anthrax infection. Antibiotic treatment is available for persons who have been exposed to anthrax or who have developed the disease.

Symptoms: Inhalation: sore throat, mild fever, muscle aches, and general malaise. Respiratory failure, shock, and meningitis often occur.

Cutaneous: a small pimple that enlarges to an ulcer that is black in the center. Fever, headache, malaise, and swollen lymph nodes can be present.

Gastrointestinal: This results from eating raw or undercooked contaminated meat. There is severe abdominal distress with fever and severe diarrhea.

Classroom Implications: Because anthrax cannot be transmitted from person to person, there is little likelihood that there will be an outbreak in the classroom. However, with anthrax being an agent of bioterrorism, be vigilant with unknown substances that may come from unusual sources. Don't open any packages or mail that may be suspicious. Contact the appropriate authorities if you suspect anthrax contamination.

Appendicitis

Background: Appendicitis is most common in adolescents and young adults but is also a major reason for abdominal surgery in children. The appendix becomes infected with bacteria normally found in the bowel. Continued inflammation may lead to abscess formation, gangrene, and perforation resulting in peritonitis.

Symptoms: steady, localized pain, usually in the lower right abdominal quadrant; constipation that began recently; nausea and vomiting; mild fever; elevated white-blood-cell count

Classroom Implications: A student returning to the classroom after an appendectomy may have restrictions on his or her activity for a time. The student may tire easily the first few days and have difficulty concentrating.

Asthma

Background: Asthma is a chronic reversible airway condition that results in recurring episodes (also called *attacks*) of breathing problems. Episodes can be triggered by upper respiratory infections (colds or flu); hard exercise; laughing or crying hard; allergies to common substances such as animal dander (tiny scales from skin), pollen, or dust; irritants such as cold air, strong smells, and chemical sprays (perfume, paint and cleaning solutions, chalk dust, lawn and turf treatments); weather changes; or tobacco smoke. During an episode the muscles surrounding the bronchial tubes tighten, thus reducing the size of the airway. The allergic response causes mucus production and a resultant productive cough. People with asthma are able to draw air into the lungs through the narrowed airway but are unable to expel carbon dioxide waste out. They may cough, wheeze, gasp for air, and feel that they are suffocating.

Symptoms: wheezing, gasping for air, hacking cough, tightness in the chest, shortness of breath

Classroom Implications: An asthma episode may be compared to taking a deep breath and not being able to let it out. A student having an asthma episode should be reassured that help is on the way. People with asthma are often fearful of the episodes. An episode may occur at any time and may be triggered by emotional strain, physical exertion, or environmental factors. Many students with asthma take prescription prevention (control) and rescue (acute) medicines, which should be available to them when needed. These medicines may cause jitteriness, overactivity, or, rarely, drowsiness. With medical management and monitoring with peak flow meters at home and school, students with asthma usually have few restrictions on activity, except during or following an acute episode.

Bronchitis (Asthmatic or Allergic)

Background: Bronchitis is inflammation of the bronchial tubes. It may develop as a result of an environmental irritant like cigarette smoke or from an upper-respiratory infection. A virus or bacterium invades the area and causes inflammation and increases mucus secretion. A deep, rumbling cough develops. Treatment is directed at drainage and expulsion of the mucus rather than at suppression of the cough.

Symptoms: chills, slight fever, back and muscle pain, sore throat, followed by dry cough and then by a cough that expels mucus

Classroom Implications: Bronchitis is a self-limiting disease in most cases; complete healing usually occurs within a few weeks. The student who has bronchitis, however, may be absent and may require help in making up missed work.

Cerebral Palsy (CP)

Background: Cerebral palsy is a term for a group of non-progressive motor disorders that impair voluntary movement. The various forms of CP are caused by developmental problems or injury to the motor areas of the central nervous system before, during, or soon after birth. Physical therapy helps many people with CP overcome their disabilities.

Symptoms: spasticity of limbs, weakness, limb deformities, speech disorders, involuntary movements, difficulty with fine movements, visual disturbances; commonly accompanied by nerve deafness, mental impairment, or seizure disorders

Classroom Implications: Students with severe CP can be mainstreamed with therapy services and support. In mild forms of CP, the symptoms may be seen only during certain activities, such as running. Students with mild CP have the usual range of intelligence and function in a regular classroom setting. Be aware of the student's particular needs, and include the student in classroom activities. Discussing the disorder with classmates and explaining why the student may sometimes move differently will increase understanding and help eliminate teasing. Drugs can be used to control seizures and muscle spasms; special braces can compensate for muscle imbalance. Surgery and mechanical aids can help to overcome impairments. Counseling and physical, occupational, speech, and behavioral therapy may be included in the student's education plan.

Diabetes

Background: Diabetes is characterized by an increase of sugar (glucose) in the blood, which also spills into the urine. In type 1 diabetes, an autoimmune disorder, cell groups in the islets of Langerhans of the pancreas no longer secrete adequate amounts of the hormone insulin. Insulin is the primary substance that allows the body to utilize sugar. In type 2 diabetes, there is a genetic predisposition to develop diabetes along with significant overweight and low physical activity that interferes with the body's use of available insulin to move sugar into the body cells, especially the muscle and fat tissue cells. There is no known cure but research is exploring pancreas cell transplantation for type 1. Optimal treatment usually consists of regulated insulin replacement (by injection or pump), self-monitoring of blood glucose, daily diet, and exercise.

Symptoms: fatigue, frequent urination, thirst, hunger, weight loss (type 1), infections that do not heal quickly

Classroom Implications: Teachers are often in a position to help identify undiagnosed diabetes. Any changes in bathroom or drinking habits should be investigated. Unexplained weight loss or the inability to concentrate or new irritability should also be suspect. A student with regulated diabetes functions normally in the classroom. If you have a student requiring insulin shots, keep a source of sugar, such as orange juice, available for low insulin (hypoglycemia) episodes. You need to accommodate a student on insulin or oral medications for type 2 diabetes who must have a snack once or twice a day at school, self-check blood glucose non-disruptively in the classroom, self-inject insulin on schedule or as the monitoring results indicate. Physical education and meal/snack time need to be coordinated.

Down Syndrome*

Background: Down syndrome is an inherited condition that is usually associated with an extra chromosome. Fifty percent of infants with the syndrome are born to mothers over the age of 35.

*Genetic conditions named for individuals are spelled without 's, as recommended by the American Society of Human Genetics.

Children with Down syndrome have a mean IQ of 50. They usually have small heads and slanted eyes. Life expectancy is normal in the absence of other birth defects, such as heart disease.

Symptoms: placidity, poor muscle tone; slanted eyes, flattened nosebridge; mouth usually held open because of enlarged tongue; short-fingered, broad hands with single crease; feet with a wide gap between the first and second toes

Classroom Implications: Children with Down syndrome often have special education resources to meet their individual needs and group activities such as Special Olympics. But many students are part of the regular classroom community. Their classmates need to understand conditions that make others different. A careful introduction to disabilities is a must for the whole class.

Epilepsy (Seizure Disorder)

Background: Epilepsy, a disorder of the nerve cells in the brain, is characterized by episodes of muscle spasms or strange sensations called seizures. The well-known kinds of generalized seizures are grand mal, petit mal, and psychomotor or temporal lobe. During a seizure, brain impulses become chaotic, causing the person to lose full consciousness and control over body movement.

Symptoms: uncontrollable jerking movements followed by a deep sleep (tonic-clonic seizure or convulsion); momentary cessation of movement (absence seizure); coordinated but strange whole body movements while in altered consciousness (simple partial or complex partial seizure)

Classroom Implications: If a student is known to have seizures, get details about the specific type, medications, and what to expect. In a tonic-clonic seizure, do not attempt to restrain the person. If the student has not fallen, gently move him or her onto the floor and move any obstructions out of the way. Do not place any objects in the student's mouth. A convulsive seizure may be a frightening experience to witness, so offer others a simple explanation and reassurance. Absence seizures, though less dramatic, make the student unresponsive with rapid blinking or other behavior; the student briefly loses consciousness. Anticonvulsive medications have side effects, such as drowsiness or making concentration difficult. Computer screens, video games, and flashing lights have been known to trigger seizures. People with epilepsy follow safety guidelines such as wearing helmets for bike riding or climbing, and swimming only with a life jacket at all times.

Hearing Loss

Background: Many conditions can produce hearing loss. Conduction deafness can be caused by sound waves being blocked by wax or by scars from middle-ear infections. It can also be caused by Eustachian tube dysfunction, middle ear fluid, or fixation of the bones of the middle ear. Most of these conditions can be reversed, and normal hearing can be restored. However, when the auditory nerve is damaged, such as by disease or prolonged loud noise, little can be done.

Symptoms: apparent inattention, frequent asking for repetition of what was said, frequent misunderstanding of verbal directions, failure to respond to normal voices or sounds, cupping of the ear to funnel sounds

Classroom Implications: Students with diagnosed hearing loss may require special seating and aids in the classroom. Some students need to wear one or two hearing aids, which should be explained to the rest of the class. Other amplification aids should be supplied when needed. If you observe changes in any student's ability to hear, make referrals for testing.

Heart Disorders

Background: Many conditions can cause heart disorders. The most common disorders in infancy and early childhood are congenital abnormalities such as valve problems, holes between right and left chambers (septal defects), and failure of an opening between the aorta and the pulmonary artery to close after birth (a condition called patent ductus arteriosus). These conditions can be surgically corrected in most instances. Another type of heart condition is a heart murmur, a series of prolonged heart sounds that can be heard as vibrations. Some murmurs are significant but most are not; they are called functional and usually disappear in time. Some significant murmurs may signal developmental heart-valve abnormalities.

Symptoms: shortness of breath, chest pain, blue tinge to the skin, fatigue, slowing of heartbeat rate, palpitations

Classroom Implications: Children who have had surgical correction for congenital heart disorders usually lead restriction-free lives. Those who have continuing problems or who develop additional problems may have to curtail physical activity, and you may need to make special plans for them. All students should be encouraged to develop good physical fitness habits and healthful eating habits to help reduce the risk for adult causes of heart disease such as high cholesterol.

Hemophilia (Bleeding Disorder)

Background: Hemophilia is one inherited bleeding disorder. Others include von Willebrand and platelet disorders. The person is unable to manufacture certain essential clotting factors and therefore might bleed to death or suffer joint damage if a cut or bruise is left untreated.

Symptoms: serious bleeding or bruising from minor injuries or normally lost tooth or heavy menstrual period

Classroom Implications: Most students who have bleeding disorders can lead normal lives if they are receiving treatment for the missing blood clotting factor. However, you should be aware of this condition and take necessary precautions to prevent injury. First-aid procedures for external and internal bleeding should be reviewed with the school nurse or with a physician. Minor episodes may be treated with a prescribed nasal spray medication.

Leukemia

Background: Leukemia is a cancer of white blood cells that eventually crowd out normal white, red, and platelet blood cells. There are several types of leukemia. Acute lymphoblastic leukemia (ALL) primarily affects children. Acute myeloid leukemia (AML) can occur in people of any age. In all people with leukemia, abnormal white blood cells form in large numbers. In children, the causes are unclear and may include genetic tendencies and conditions such as Down syndrome.

Symptoms: high fever and joint pain; bleeding from the mouth, nose, kidneys, and large intestine; enlarged liver, spleen, and lymph nodes

Classroom Implications: Continual improvement in chemotherapy has made remissions (absences of any signs of the disease) much more common, especially in acute lymphoblastic leukemia. Students undergoing treatment for leukemia may be able to return to school after the acute stage of the disease has been arrested. However, depending on the treatment schedule, they may have to return to the hospital periodically. Every effort to maintain continuity in the classroom for these students should be made. Many of the drugs that are administered cause hair loss, which should be explained to the rest of the class. Sometimes students become frightened by the word cancer, and questions such as "Can I catch it?" "Will he die?" and "Will I die?" may be asked. Dealing with these types of concerns openly and honestly may alleviate fear and anxiety.

Lyme Disease

Background: Lyme disease is caused by a spirochete that is transmitted to humans by deer ticks.

Symptoms: After 3 to 32 days from a tick bite exposure (lasting 12 or more hours), a skin lesion begins as a red spot or bump, but enlarges to look like a "bull's eye." Other signs are flu-like tiredness, chills, muscle and joint pain, and swollen lymph glands. Complications include joint arthritis, Bell's palsy, and heart rate irregularities.

Classroom Implications: Persons conducting school outings in areas infested by ticks should instruct students to wear protective clothing and to check hourly for ticks. Any ticks should be removed with an appropriate technique and the site cleaned.

Muscular Dystrophy

Background: The muscular dystrophies are a group of inherited progressive diseases that produce a breakdown in the muscle fibers, causing increasing weakness and difficulty with movement and breathing. Duchenne muscular dystrophy is the most common form. It occurs in boys 3 to 7 years of age. The disease causes a steady increase in muscle weakness, and most patients use a wheelchair by the age of 10 or 12.

Symptoms: muscle weakness causing a waddling gait, toe-walking, a swaybacked appearance, frequent falls, difficulty in standing up and in climbing stairs

Classroom Implications: Many children with muscular dystrophy, especially the less common, milder forms, are mainstreamed. If one of your students has muscular dystrophy, you need to be aware of his or her specific progression and limitations. Special equipment along with physical and occupational therapy may be needed for instruction and for support. Fostering understanding among classmates is of utmost importance.

Peptic Ulcer

Background: A peptic (stomach) ulcer is a sore or hole in the stomach or the first part of the small intestine (duodenum). It used to be thought that a peptic ulcer was a chronic disease that resulted from the overproduction of gastric juices manufactured by the stomach to break down foods. However, in the mid-1980s it was discovered that most ulcers may be caused by a bacterium, *Helicobacter pylori*. These ulcers can be cured with antibiotics. The course of treatment lasts for two weeks and can permanently cure the ulcer. Peptic ulcers are relatively common among adults, though they do occur in children, even before the age of 10.

Symptoms: a painful burning sensation, usually relieved by meals and occurring at night; nausea and vomiting if the pain is severe; constipation; anemia

Classroom Implications: Students who complain of persistent, localized stomach pain should see a physician. Most often a course of antibiotics will be prescribed.

Reye's Syndrome

Background: The cause of Reye's syndrome is currently unknown. Reye's syndrome (RS) is primarily a children's disease, although it can occur at any age. It affects all organs of the body but is most harmful to the brain and the liver—causing an acute increase of pressure within the brain and, often, massive accumulations of fat in the liver and other organs. The disorder commonly occurs during recovery from a viral infection, although it can also develop 3 to 5 days after the onset of the viral illness (most commonly influenza or chicken pox). The cause of RS remains a mystery. However, studies have shown that using aspirin or salicylate-containing medications to treat viral illnesses increases the risk of developing RS.

Symptoms: uncontrollable nausea and vomiting about the sixth day after a viral infection; noticeable change in mental function; lethargy, mild amnesia, disorientation, agitation, unresponsiveness, coma, seizures, fixed and dilated pupils

Classroom Implications: Parents should be informed of the possible link between aspirin and Rèye's syndrome. Some people recover completely, while others may sustain varying degrees of brain damage. The syndrome may leave permanent neurological damage, causing mental retardation or problems with movement.

Rheumatic Fever

Background: Rheumatic fever is a possible secondary complication of a streptococcal infection, especially strep throat. Rheumatic fever is an acute inflammatory reaction to the streptococcal bacterium and can affect one or more major sites, including the joints, the brain, the heart, and the skin. The disease is rare before 4 years of age and uncommon after age 18.

Symptoms: varied symptoms appearing alone or in combination after a severe sore throat: a flat, painless rash, lasting less than a day; painless nodules on the legs; swollen tender joints; recurrent fevers; movement disorders.

Classroom Implications: Since rheumatic fever can develop to varying degrees, the amount of physical restriction depends on the joint and cardiac problems of the individual. Psychological problems have been noted in students who have been restricted from play because they have rheumatic fever. It is important for all parents and school personnel to see that a student with a possible strep infection is treated promptly. Any changes in a student's work habits, appearance, or energy level after a strep infection should be investigated.

Rheumatoid Arthritis

Background: Rheumatoid arthritis is a chronic autoimmune disorder characterized by inflammation of the joints. The immune system, for unknown reasons, attacks a person's own cells inside the joint capsule. White blood cells travel to the synovium and cause a reaction. As rheumatoid arthritis progresses, these abnormal synovial cells destroy the cartilage and bone within the joint. The surrounding muscles, ligaments, and tendons that support and stabilize the joint become weak.

In children the knees, elbows, wrists, and other large joints tend to be affected. This may result in interference with growth and development. In some cases the eyes and heart are affected. Complete remission is more likely in children than in adults.

Symptoms: rash, fever, inflammation of the irises, enlargement of the spleen and lymph nodes; swelling, pain, and tenderness of the involved joints

Classroom Implications: A student with rheumatoid arthritis may be absent frequently because of the chronic, recurring nature of the disease and may need help in keeping up with schoolwork. Stiffness of joints and possible deformities may limit the student's movement. Restrictions on the student's activity can be less burdensome if you explain the situation to the whole class. Emotional support from classmates can contribute to the student's sense of well being. Care usually includes healthy lifestyle (diet, exercise, and rest), stress management, medications for pain and inflammation, and sometimes joint surgery.

Scoliosis

Background: Scoliosis is a lateral curvature of the spine. This disorder occurs most commonly during the adolescent growth period. It is estimated that between 5 and 10 percent of school age children have a single or double spinal curvature in varying degrees. However, only about 2 percent of the cases are significant. The effect of scoliosis depends on its severity, how early it is detected, and treatment adherence. The curve usually does not get worse once the spine has reached full growth. Scoliosis is more common among girls than boys.

Symptoms: unequal shoulder levels, a hunchbacked appearance (kyphosis or C-shaped curve), fatigue or muscle aches in the lower back region, persistent back pain

Classroom Implications: Many states now require scoliosis screening for preadolescent and adolescent students. Treatment of scoliosis may range from monitoring to muscle development exercises, to bracing, or to corrective surgery. Special braces or casts can threaten a teenager's self-concept. Therefore, counseling and support from teachers, parents, and peers are very important in treating a youngster with scoliosis.

Sickle-Cell Anemia

Background: Sickle-cell anemia is an inherited disease that affects African Americans mainly but not exclusively. Anemias are conditions in which the blood is low in red blood cells or in hemoglobin, causing a decrease in the body's ability to transport oxygen to all cells. This disease is named after the abnormal, sickle shape of some red blood cells that was a protective adaptation to fight malaria. Because of their shape these cells are not able to flow easily through the capillaries and tend to jam up around joints and in organs. This inhibiting of blood flow can cause acute pain.

Symptoms: fatigue, painful crises when blood vessels are blocked, yellow skin and eyes (jaundice), enlarged spleen, poor growth and delayed puberty, vision abnormalities

Classroom Implications: Sickle-cell anemia can cause repeated painful crisis situations that may require hospital treatment. A student with the disease may be out of school frequently and will need help in completing schoolwork and maintaining contact with the class. Support students' self-care which includes drinking extra water, pain medicines at school, moderate exercise, diet rich in folic acid, avoiding extreme cold and heat, and avoiding exposure to infections.

Sty

Background: Sties are inflamed hair follicles or glands on the eyelids. They are usually caused by staphylococcal bacteria.

Symptoms: a tiny abcess on the eyelid, redness, tenderness of the eyelid, sensitivity to light, the feeling of having a foreign body in the eye

Classroom Implications: Students who develop sties should be referred to the school nurse and may improve with the application of warm compresses. If not improved in 2–3 days, referral to a physician is indicated. Sties are not contagious.

Tendonitis

Background: Tendonitis is an inflammation of the tendons surrounding various joints (shoulder, elbow, wrist, and knee most often). The inflammation usually results from a joint being forced beyond its normal range of motion or in an abnormal direction. Excessive exercise or repeated injury to a joint may also cause tendonitis. A common form of tendonitis, tennis elbow, results from the excessive rotation of the forearm and hand while playing tennis. The muscles of the forearm are strained, and the inflammation spreads to the elbow.

Symptoms: swelling, local tenderness, disabling pain when the affected joint is moved

Classroom Implications: Students may develop tendonitis from excessive periods of repeated exercise such as pitching a baseball or hitting a tennis ball. Students who spend many hours working the levers of video games may experience tendonitis of the wrist joint. Tendonitis may often be prevented through proper coaching in technique and appropriate periods of rest. Cross-training mixes impact-loading exercise, such as running, with lower-impact exercise, such as biking or swimming. Students who complain of constant, disabling pain in any joint should be referred for medical evaluation.

Tetanus (Lockjaw)

Background: Tetanus is an acute infectious disease caused by a bacterium that produces spores and that can live in an environment without oxygen, namely soil or animal feces. Once the toxin from the bacterium enters the body, it interferes with the central nervous system's ability to transmit impulses

correctly. This causes a generalized spasticity and intermittent convulsive movements. Stiffness of the jaw is a classic symptom of tetanus (hence the name lockjaw). The typical route of transmission is through a skin wound, usually a dirty splinter or puncture wound, such as from a knife or nail that has been contaminated with dirt containing the spores. The spores then develop into bacteria that release the toxin. Primary immunization against tetanus begins in infancy with a booster at school age. This is given in the form of a DTaP (diphtheria-tetanus-acellular pertussis) combination vaccine. After that, booster injections should be administered every 10 years lifelong.

Symptoms: stiff jaw muscles and difficulty in swallowing; restlessness and irritability; stiffness in the neck, arms, or legs; headache, fever, sore throat, chills, convulsions

Classroom Implications: Help students clean all wounds promptly and thoroughly to prevent exposure. If a student suffers a deep wound and has not had a tetanus booster within five years, his/her doctor may order a booster within two days. Following first aid, all wounds of concern should be reported to the school nurse for proper evaluation.

Vision Disorders

Background: There are three common eye disorders that produce errors in refraction and that decrease visual acuity. The most common childhood disorder is farsightedness (hyperopia), which interferes with the ability to see clearly things that are nearby. In nearsightedness (myopia) a person is able to see things clearly that are near, but distance vision is impaired. Astigmatism, or distorted vision, occurs when there are defective curvatures of the refractive surfaces of the cornea. Other conditions such as eye muscle imbalance also interfere with clear binocular vision. Young children may suppress poorer vision in one eye and, if not treated, in preschool years may permanently lose the vision in that eye (developing amblyopia).

Symptoms: head tilt, squinting, headaches, eye muscle fatigue, holding reading material unusually close or far away, complaining of not being able to see the board, inability to do fine motor or sport tasks as well as expected for age and overall development.

Classroom Implications: Make sure vision screening and any referrals are completed as soon as possible to limit the risk of amblyopia. Students with undiagnosed eye disorders may have a difficult time with schoolwork. As a teacher you are in an excellent position to note such problems and to make appropriate referrals. Reinforce wearing and care for glasses as prescribed, and refer families that need community resources to get needed glasses (not usually covered by health insurance).

West Nile Virus

Background: The West Nile virus (WNV) was first known in 1937 and is in the family Flavivirus, related to the type that causes St. Louis encephalitis. WNV arrived in the US about 1999 through imported animals and objects. Generally, WNV is spread by the bite of an infected mosquito. Mosquitoes harbor the virus in the salivary glands after feeding on infected birds. Infected mosquitoes can then spread WNV to humans and other animals they bite.

Symptoms: WNV affects the central nervous system. Most people (80 percent) will not show any symptoms. Up to 20 percent will have mild symptoms for a few days, including fever, headache, body aches, nausea, vomiting, and sometimes swollen lymph glands or a skin rash (trunk). About one in 150

people infected with WNV will develop severe illness: high fever, headache, neck stiffness, coma, tremors, convulsions, muscle weakness, vision loss, numbness, and paralysis. These symptoms may last several weeks, and neurological effects may be permanent.

Classroom Implications: The best way to avoid WNV is to prevent mosquito bites. School buildings should have good screens on windows and doors. Get rid of mosquito breeding sites by emptying standing water. Drill drainage holes in tire swings so water drains out. Keep children's wading pools empty and on their sides when not being used. During activities, precautions should be taken. When outdoors, use insect repellents containing DEET (N, N-diethyl-meta-toluamide). Wear long sleeves and pants.

School-Home Connection

A Note to Family Members

What We Are Learning About Health

In Chapter 1 of *Harcourt Health and Fitness,* we are learning about

- the interdependence, structure, and function of body organs.
- stages of human growth and the effects of environment and heredity on growth, with an emphasis on puberty.
- steps for resolving conflicts over a child's growing sense of independence.
- building a reputation of trustworthiness.

 Visit **www.harcourtschool.com/health** for links to parent resources.

How You Can Help

Parental involvement in the school environment is part of a coordinated school health plan that includes the home, school, community, and social services. You can support your school through increased communication and by volunteering your time or talents. At home you can support your child's learning by

- discussing how you felt as you went through the stages of growth.
- encouraging your child to let you know when a family conflict needs resolution.
- examining ways your child can build a good reputation with others.

A Family Activity

As people grow, they pass through several stages. Talk with your child about major events that have affected his or her development during two stages—infancy and childhood. Work together to record these events in the following table. For the sections entitled "Adolescence" and "Adulthood," help your child anticipate some of the major events that he or she may experience during these stages, such as graduation from high school or full-time employment.

Stages of Growth

	Events in Your Life
Infancy	
Childhood	
Adolescence	
Adulthood	

La escuela y la casa

Nota para los familiares

Lo que estamos aprendiendo acerca de la Salud

En el Capítulo 1 de *Harcourt Health and Fitness* estamos aprendiendo acerca de:

• La función, estructura e interdependencia de los órganos del cuerpo humano.
• Las etapas del crecimiento y la influencia del medio ambiente y de los factores hereditarios en el crecimiento, especialmente durante la pubertad.
• Los pasos necesarios para resolver los conflictos que se presentan a medida que el niño busca más independencia.
• Cómo demostrar que se es digno de confianza.

 Visite **www.harcourtschool.com/health** para encontrar enlaces con recursos en inglés para los padres.

Cómo puede usted ayudar

La participación familiar en las actividades escolares forma parte de un plan de salud organizado que incluye la casa, la escuela, la comunidad y los servicios sociales. Usted puede apoyar a la escuela manteniendo una buena comunicación y ofreciendo su tiempo y sus talentos como voluntario. En casa, usted puede apoyar el aprendizaje de su hijo(a) haciendo lo siguiente:

• Háblele de sus emociones durante las diferentes etapas de su crecimiento.
• Anímelo a que le informe cuando necesita que un conflicto familiar se resuelva.
• Busquen maneras en que su hijo(a) pueda establecer una buena reputación y volverse una persona confiable.

Actividad familiar

Todos pasamos por diferentes etapas mientras crecemos. Hable con su hijo(a) sobre la influencia que han tenido en su desarrollo los eventos importantes ocurridos durante su infancia y niñez. Ayúdele a escribir la información en la tabla de abajo. Para las secciones de "Adolescencia" y "Edad adulta", piensen en aquellos eventos que muy posiblemente influirán en su vida, como la graduación de la escuela secundaria o un trabajo de tiempo completo.

Etapas del crecimiento

	Sucesos importantes en su vida
Infancia	
Niñez	
Adolescencia	
Edad adulta	

© Harcourt

Name _____   Date _____

School-Home Connection

A Note to Family Members

What We Are Learning About Health

In Chapter 2 of *Harcourt Health and Fitness,* we are learning about

- the importance of personal hygiene as children get older.
- how the eyes and ears function and ways to keep them healthy.
- communicating with family members to reach acceptable compromises.
- developing self-confidence through activities that build self-respect, such as grooming and good hygiene.

 Visit **www.harcourtschool.com/health** for links to parent resources.

How You Can Help

Parental involvement in the school environment is part of a coordinated school health plan that includes the home, school, community, and social services. You can support your school through increased communication and by volunteering your time or talents. At home you can support your child's learning by

- discussing your own good hygiene habits.
- examining the need for healthy eyes and ears.
- praising his or her efforts to compromise in a reasonable manner.

A Family Activity

People use a variety of products each day to protect and care for their skin, hair, nails, teeth, vision, and hearing. During your next trip to the supermarket or pharmacy, ask your child to list the different kinds of health-care products on the shelves. Have your child record his or her findings in the following table. After the table has been completed, discuss which category has the most health-care products, and why.

Health-Care Products

Skin	Hair	Nails	Teeth	Eyes	Ears

© Harcourt

Chapter 2 • Being a Wise Health Consumer

La escuela y la casa

Nota para los familiares

Lo que estamos aprendiendo acerca de la Salud

En el Capítulo 2 de *Harcourt Health and Fitness* estamos aprendiendo acerca de:

- La importancia de desarrollar buenos hábitos de higiene personal mientras crecemos.
- Cómo trabajan los ojos y los oídos y cómo mantenerlos sanos.
- La comunicación en familia para lograr acuerdos sobre metas posibles.
- El cuidado e higiene personal como unas de las maneras de adquirir seguridad propia y autorespeto.

 Visite **www.harcourtschool.com/health** para encontrar enlaces con recursos en inglés para los padres.

Cómo puede usted ayudar

La participación familiar en las actividades escolares forma parte de un plan de salud organizado que incluye la casa, la escuela, la comunidad y los servicios sociales. Usted puede apoyar a la escuela manteniendo una buena comunicación y ofreciendo su tiempo y sus talentos como voluntario. En casa, usted puede apoyar el aprendizaje de su hijo(a) haciendo lo siguiente:

- Háblele sobre sus propios hábitos de higiene.
- Comenten acerca de la importancia de mantener los ojos y los oídos sanos.
- Elógielo cuando demuestre que se esfuerza por llegar a acuerdos razonables.

Actividad familiar

Las personas usan diariamente una gran variedad de productos para el cuidado de la piel, el cabello, las uñas, los dientes, los ojos y los oídos. Cuando vayan al supermercado, pida a su hijo que haga una lista de los diferentes productos de salud e higiene que vea y que los escriba en la tabla de abajo cuando llegue a la casa. Una vez llene la tabla, hablen sobre la categoría que tenga más productos.

Productos de cuidado personal

Piel	Cabello	Uñas	Dientes	Ojos	Oídos

© Harcourt

School-Home Connection

A Note to Family Members

What We Are Learning About Health

In Chapter 3 of *Harcourt Health and Fitness,* we are learning about

- the basic nutrients in food and how the body gets and uses these nutrients.
- using MyPyramid to recognize a balanced diet that includes proper portions and energy balance.
- avoiding food poisoning through proper handling and storage of food.
- showing self-control and responsibility when choosing foods.

 Visit **www.harcourtschool.com/health** for links to parent resources.

How You Can Help

Parental involvement in the school environment is part of a coordinated school health plan that includes the home, school, community, and social services. You can support your school through increased communication and by volunteering your time or talents. At home you can support your child's learning by

- reviewing MyPyramid together.
- encouraging your child to help in the kitchen to learn food handling techniques.
- practicing making healthful food choices.

A Family Activity

As children mature, they make more decisions about the foods they eat each day. Ask your child to write, in the spaces below, what foods make up his or her favorite breakfast, lunch, and dinner. Then ask your child to record the food group to which each item belongs. Examine the table with your child. Ask your child if the three meals represent a balanced diet. If not, discuss ways in which your child might make healthful changes.

Your Favorite Meals

Meal	Food Groups
Breakfast	
Lunch	
Dinner	

La escuela y la casa

Lo que estamos aprendiendo acerca de la Salud

En el Capítulo 3 de *Harcourt Health and Fitness* estamos aprendiendo acerca de:

• Los nutrientes de los alimentos y la forma como el cuerpo los absorbe y los usa.
• Cómo usar MiPirámide para identificar una dieta balanceada que incluya las porciones adecuadas y un balance energético.
• Formas de preparar y guardar los alimentos para evitar intoxicaciones.
• La responsabilidad y el autocontrol al alimentarnos.

 Visite **www.harcourtschool.com/health** para encontrar enlaces con recursos en inglés para los padres.

Cómo puede usted ayudar

La participación familiar en las actividades escolares forma parte de un plan de salud organizado que incluye la casa, la escuela, la comunidad y los servicios sociales. Usted puede apoyar a la escuela manteniendo una buena comunicación y ofreciendo su tiempo y sus talentos como voluntario. En casa, usted puede apoyar el aprendizaje de su hijo(a) haciendo lo siguiente:

• Estudien MiPirámide.
• Anímelo a ayudar en la cocina para que vea cómo se prepara y guarda la comida.
• Practiquen nuevas formas de escoger alimentos saludables.

Actividad familiar

Los niños toman cada vez más decisiones sobre lo que comen a medida que crecen. Pida a su hijo(a) que describa su desayuno, almuerzo y cena favoritos en la tabla de abajo. Luego, pídale que escriba el nombre del grupo al que cada alimento pertenezca. Cuando termine, examinen juntos la tabla. Pregúntele si cree que las tres comidas que escribió representan una dieta balanceada. Si no lo es, hablen sobre los cambios que necesita hacer para obtenerla.

Mis comidas favoritas

Comida	Grupo de alimentos
Desayuno	
Almuerzo	
Cena	

Name _____   Date _____

School-Home Connection

A Note to Family Members

What We Are Learning About Health

In Chapter 4 of *Harcourt Health and Fitness,* we are learning about

- how food, activity, and sleep affect overall health.
- safe exercise that helps various body systems, such as the respiratory and circulatory systems.
- setting goals to be physically active, personally and with the family.
- showing fairness by following the rules of games and by respecting other players.

 Visit **www.harcourtschool.com/health** for links to parent resources.

How You Can Help

Parental involvement in the school environment is part of a coordinated school health plan that includes the home, school, community, and social services. You can support your school through increased communication and by volunteering your time or talents. At home you can support your child's learning by

- emphasizing the proper balance of diet, exercise, and sleep as your child grows.
- encouraging your child to be more physically active.
- examining the rules of a favorite sport or game.

A Family Activity

Physical fitness can be a family goal. With your child, discuss some ways in which members of your family might exercise together. Help your child understand the limitations and needs of family members. Ask your child to write his or her ideas in the table below. An example has been provided. After the table has been completed, hold a family meeting to discuss your child's ideas.

Exercising Together

Description of Exercise	Names of Family Members
Do stretches or sit-ups while watching TV	Mom and Jason

La escuela y la casa

Nota para los familiares

Lo que estamos aprendiendo acerca de la Salud

En el Capítulo 4 de *Harcourt Health and Fitness* estamos aprendiendo acerca de:

- Cómo la alimentación, la actividad y el sueño influyen en la salud.
- Los ejercicios adecuados para el buen funcionamiento de los sistemas del cuerpo humano, como el respiratorio y el digestivo.
- Cómo establecer metas adecuadas para mantenerse activo físicamente, tanto a nivel personal como familiar.
- La importancia de obedecer las reglas en los juegos y respetar a los otros jugadores.

Cómo puede usted ayudar

La participación familiar en las actividades escolares forma parte de un plan de salud organizado que incluye la casa, la escuela, la comunidad y los servicios sociales. Usted puede apoyar a la escuela manteniendo una buena comunicación y ofreciendo su tiempo y sus talentos como voluntario. En casa, usted puede apoyar el aprendizaje de su hijo(a) haciendo lo siguiente:

- Háblele sobre la importancia de seguir una dieta balanceada, así como hacer ejercicio y dormir adecuadamente.
- Anímelo a participar en más actividades físicas.
- Examinen las reglas de uno de sus juegos o deportes favoritos.

Visite **www.harcourtschool.com/health** para encontrar enlaces con recursos en inglés para los padres.

Actividad familiar

Una buena meta familiar podría ser alcanzar un buen estado físico. Hablen sobre las diferentes maneras en que pueden hacer ejercicio en familia. Ayude a su hijo(a) a entender cualquier limitación o necesidad física que exista en la familia. Luego, pídale que escriba sus ideas en la tabla de abajo, siguiendo el ejemplo. Cuando haya terminado de llenar la tabla, reúnanse en familia para comentar las ideas de su hijo.

Hagamos ejercicio juntos

Descripción del ejercicio	Nombre de los familiares
Estiramiento o abdominales mientras ven TV	Mami y Jaime

Name _____   Date _____

School-Home Connection

A Note to Family Members

What We Are Learning About Health

In Chapter 5 of *Harcourt Health and Fitness,* we are learning about

- situations inside and outside the home that could lead to injury.
- applying first aid to serious and minor injuries when responding to emergency situations.
- making the correct decisions about personal safety.
- caring for someone who has been injured, both at the time of injury and afterward.

 Visit **www.harcourtschool.com/health** for links to parent resources.

How You Can Help

Parental involvement in the school environment is part of a coordinated school health plan that includes the home, school, community, and social services. You can support your school through increased communication and by volunteering your time or talents. At home you can support your child's learning by

- discussing situations that could lead to injury in your child's daily life.

- encouraging your child to learn emergency first aid.

- praising your child when he or she comforts or cares for an injured friend or family member.

A Family Activity

Regular fire drills are an important part of home safety. In the space provided, have your child identify one or two escape routes from each room in your home. Continue the list on a separate sheet of paper. Hold a family meeting to discuss the routes and identify a location where the family should gather after escaping from the house during a fire.

Fire Escape Routes

Room	Route

La escuela y la casa

Nota para los familiares

Lo que estamos aprendiendo acerca de la Salud

En el Capítulo 5 de *Harcourt Health and Fitness* estamos aprendiendo acerca de:

- Las actividades que pueden causar lesiones dentro y fuera de la casa.
- Primeros auxilios para lesiones menores y graves durante una emergencia.
- Cómo tomar decisiones correctas sobre la seguridad personal.
- Cómo cuidar de un herido durante y después de un accidente.

 Visite **www.harcourtschool.com/health** para encontrar enlaces con recursos en inglés para los padres.

Cómo puede usted ayudar

La participación familiar en las actividades escolares forma parte de un plan de salud organizado que incluye la casa, la escuela, la comunidad y los servicios sociales. Usted puede apoyar a la escuela manteniendo una buena comunicación y ofreciendo su tiempo y sus talentos como voluntario. En casa, usted puede apoyar el aprendizaje de su hijo(a) haciendo lo siguiente:

- Hablen sobre las actividades de la vida diaria que pueden resultar peligrosas y causar lesiones.
- Anime a su hijo a aprender primeros auxilios.
- Elógielo cuando participa en el cuidado de un amigo o familiar que se ha lesionado.

Actividad familiar

Los simulacros de incendio son una práctica importante para la seguridad en el hogar. Pida a su hijo que describa rutas de escape desde cada habitación de su casa, en la tabla de abajo. Si necesita, puede continuar la lista en otra hoja. Hagan una reunión en la que toda la familia pueda hablar sobre las rutas de escape y establecer un punto exterior de encuentro en caso de que tengan que salir rápidamente durante un incendio.

Rutas de escape

Habitación	Ruta

Name _____ Date _____

School-Home Connection

A Note to Family Members

What We Are Learning About Health

In Chapter 6 of *Harcourt Health and Fitness,* we are learning about

- recognizing and responding to violence and threatening situations.
- what to do when someone has a weapon or is threatening.
- positive communication skills that could help avoid potential violence.
- being fair by practicing effective listening skills.

 Visit **www.harcourtschool.com/health** for links to parent resources.

How You Can Help

Parental involvement in the school environment is part of a coordinated school health plan that includes the home, school, community, and social services. You can support your school through increased communication and by volunteering your time or talents. At home you can support your child's learning by

- discussing situations that could lead to violence.
- emphasizing the importance of preventing potentially violent situations.
- role-playing effective listening and communication with another person.

A Family Activity

Violence can happen anywhere at any time. Children today need to know what to do in these types of situations. After your child has reviewed this chapter, test his or her knowledge by having him or her fill out the table below of ways to avoid violence. Encourage your child to come up with other circumstances that might be encountered and the ways he or she would deal with those situations.

Avoiding Violence

Situation	What to Do
Being threatened	
Finding a weapon	
An act of terrorism	
A fight at school	
Seeing dangerous people while alone	

© Harcourt

La escuela y la casa

Nota para los familiares

Lo que estamos aprendiendo acerca de la Salud

En el Capítulo 6 de *Harcourt Health and Fitness* estamos aprendiendo acerca de:

- Cómo identificar situaciones peligrosas y violentas y actuar adecuadamente.
- Qué hacer cuando alguien tiene un arma o constituye una amenaza.
- La importancia de la buena comunicación como una forma de evitar situaciones violentas.
- La importancia de escuchar lo que otros dicen y obrar con imparcialidad.

 Visite **www.harcourtschool.com/health** para encontrar enlaces con recursos en inglés para los padres.

Cómo puede usted ayudar

La participación familiar en las actividades escolares forma parte de un plan de salud organizado que incluye la casa, la escuela, la comunidad y los servicios sociales. Usted puede apoyar a la escuela manteniendo una buena comunicación y ofreciendo su tiempo y sus talentos como voluntario. En casa, usted puede apoyar el aprendizaje de su hijo(a) haciendo lo siguiente:

- Hablen sobre las actividades que pueden desencadenar situaciones violentas.
- Resalte la importancia de prevenir circunstancias violentas.
- Improvisen situaciones en las que tengan que comunicarse eficazmente con otras personas.

Actividad familiar

Los actos de violencia puede surgir en cualquier momento y en cualquier lugar. Por esta razón, los niños deben saber cómo actuar cuando se vean afectados. Pida a su hijo(a) que repase el contenido del capítulo y que llene la tabla de abajo. Pídale que añada otras situaciones que crea que podrían surgir y escriba lo que haría.

Cómo evitar la violencia

Situación	Lo que debo hacer
Cuando alguien me amenaza	
Si encuentro un arma	
En un atentado terrorista	
En una pelea en la escuela	
Si veo personas sospechosas y estoy solo	

© Harcourt

School-Home Connection

A Note to Family Members

What We Are Learning About Health

In Chapter 7 of *Harcourt Health and Fitness,* we are learning about

- causes and symptoms of communicable and noncommunicable diseases.
- the function of the body's immune system.
- helping prevent disease by managing stress through positive thinking and relaxation.
- taking responsibility for your own well-being as you get older.

 Visit **www.harcourtschool.com/health** for links to parent resources.

How You Can Help

Parental involvement in the school environment is part of a coordinated school health plan that includes the home, school, community, and social services. You can support your school through increased communication and by volunteering your time or talents. At home you can support your child's learning by

- talking about how a disease has affected someone you know.
- reviewing ways to maintain and support the body's immune system.
- praising your child's efforts to take control of his or her own wellness.

A Family Activity

Heredity plays a role in a number of diseases. Doctors routinely ask if there is a history of certain diseases in a patient's family. Work with your child to fill out the following table of diseases in your family. In the proper column, indicate if anyone in your family has had the disease named on the left. This information will not be shared in class.

Family History

Disease	Father's Side	Mother's Side
Heart disease		
Cancer		
Diabetes		
Other		

La escuela y la casa

Nota para los familiares

Lo que estamos aprendiendo acerca de la Salud

En el Capítulo 7 de *Harcourt Health and Fitness* estamos aprendiendo acerca de:

- Las causas y síntomas de las enfermedades contagiosas y no contagiosas.
- La función del sistema inmunitario.
- Cómo manejar el estrés y prevenir las enfermedades mediante la relajación y una actitud positiva.
- La necesidad de asumir la responsabilidad por nuestro bienestar a medida de crecemos.

 Visite **www.harcourtschool.com/health** para encontrar enlaces con recursos en inglés para los padres.

Cómo puede usted ayudar

La participación familiar en las actividades escolares forma parte de un plan de salud organizado que incluye la casa, la escuela, la comunidad y los servicios sociales. Usted puede apoyar a la escuela manteniendo una buena comunicación y ofreciendo su tiempo y sus talentos como voluntario. En casa, usted puede apoyar el aprendizaje de su hijo(a) haciendo lo siguiente:

- Hablen sobre la forma como una enfermedad ha afectado a alguien que conozcan.
- Repasen las maneras de mantener un buen sistema inmunitario.
- Elógielo cuando demuestre que se está responsabilizando por su propio bienestar.

Actividad familiar

Los factores hereditarios influyen en muchas enfermedades, por eso los médicos siempre preguntan si existen ciertas enfermedades en la familia. Ayude a su hijo(a) a llenar la información que pide la tabla de abajo, escribiendo en la columna respectiva el nombre del familiar que tiene esa enfermedad. Esta información es privada y no se va a divulgar en la clase.

Historia familiar

Enfermedad	Por parte del padre	Por parte de la madre
Enfermedades del corazón		
Cáncer		
Diabetes		
Otra		

© Harcourt

Name _____   Date _____

School-Home Connection

A Note to Family Members

What We Are Learning About Health

In Chapter 8 of *Harcourt Health and Fitness,* we are learning about

- use of medicines and the effects they have on the body.
- the harmful effects and safe avoidance of illegal drugs.
- refusing illegal drugs.
- being trustworthy about not using drugs.

 Visit **www.harcourtschool.com/health** for links to parent resources.

How You Can Help

Parental involvement in the school environment is part of a coordinated school health plan that includes the home, school, community, and social services. You can support your school through increased communication and by volunteering your time or talents. At home you can support your child's learning by

- explaining how you have been helped by safe and effective use of medicines.

- discussing the use of illegal drugs in your own community.

- role-playing with your child proper ways to refuse illegal drugs.

A Family Activity

Prescription and over-the-counter medicines have expiration dates printed on their labels. Look through your family's medicines with your child. (You may want to perform this step on your own to help respect the privacy of family members.) Then, in the space provided, have your child write the name, type, and expiration date of each medicine. Review the table with other family members. Decide which medicines should be discarded now or at some time in the future.

Home Medicine Inventory

Name of Medicine	Prescription or OTC	Expiration Date

La escuela y la casa

Nota para los familiares

Lo que estamos aprendiendo acerca de la Salud

En el Capítulo 8 de *Harcourt Health and Fitness* estamos aprendiendo acerca de:

- Los medicamentos y sus efectos en el cuerpo.
- Los efectos dañinos de las drogas ilegales.
- Cómo rechazar las drogas ilegales.
- La importancia de ser responsable con respecto al consumo de drogas.

 Visite **www.harcourtschool.com/health** para encontrar enlaces con recursos en inglés para los padres.

Cómo puede usted ayudar

La participación familiar en las actividades escolares forma parte de un plan de salud organizado que incluye la casa, la escuela, la comunidad y los servicios sociales. Usted puede apoyar a la escuela manteniendo una buena comunicación y ofreciendo su tiempo y sus talentos como voluntario. En casa, usted puede apoyar el aprendizaje de su hijo(a) haciendo lo siguiente:

- Explíquele cómo los medicamentos lo han ayudado a usted.
- Hablen sobre el consumo de drogas ilegales en su comunidad.
- Improvisen diferentes maneras de rechazar las drogas ilegales.

Actividad familiar

Todos los medicamentos tienen una fecha de vencimiento escrita en su empaque. Ayude a su hijo(a) a buscar medicamentos en la casa, o hágalo usted mismo si desea guardar la privacidad de algún miembro de la familia. Luego, pídale que llene la información que se pide en la tabla para cada una de los medicamentos que encuentren. Revise la información con otros familiares para determinar si se deben deshacer de algunos de esos medicamentos.

Inventario de medicamentos de la casa

Nombre del medicamento	¿Con receta o sin receta?	Fecha de vencimiento

Name _____   Date _____

School-Home Connection

A Note to Family Members

What We Are Learning About Health

In Chapter 9 of *Harcourt Health and Fitness,* we are learning about

- alcohol and tobacco and the risks of using them.
- reasons people would use tobacco or alcohol.
- practicing dealing with peer pressure to use alcohol.
- building good citizenship by respecting people in positions of authority.

 Visit **www.harcourtschool.com/health** for links to parent resources.

How You Can Help

Parental involvement in the school environment is part of a coordinated school health plan that includes the home, school, community, and social services. You can support your school through increased communication and by volunteering your time or talents. At home you can support your child's learning by

- discussing the use of alcohol and tobacco in your community.
- praising your child for refusing negative peer pressure.
- explaining to your child who a person in authority is.

A Family Activity

With your child, research local support groups that provide help for problem drinkers and their families. Such groups include Alcoholics Anonymous, Al-Anon, Alateen, and Adult Children of Alcoholics. Look in the Yellow Pages of the local telephone book, read local newspapers to find ads, or call a local hospital. Ask your child to enter the findings in the following table.

Local Support Groups

Name of Group	Where	When	Phone Number

© Harcourt

La escuela y la casa

Nota para los familiares

Lo que estamos aprendiendo acerca de la Salud

En el Capítulo 9 de *Harcourt Health and Fitness* estamos aprendiendo acerca de:

- El consumo de tabaco y alcohol y sus riesgos.
- Las razones por las que las personas consumen tabaco y alcohol.
- Cómo manejar la presión de los compañeros acerca del uso del alcohol.
- Las maneras de actuar como un buen ciudadano al respetar a quienes tienen autoridad.

 Visite **www.harcourtschool.com/health** para encontrar enlaces con recursos en inglés para los padres.

Cómo puede usted ayudar

La participación familiar en las actividades escolares forma parte de un plan de salud organizado que incluye la casa, la escuela, la comunidad y los servicios sociales. Usted puede apoyar a la escuela manteniendo una buena comunicación y ofreciendo su tiempo y sus talentos como voluntario. En casa, usted puede apoyar el aprendizaje de su hijo(a) haciendo lo siguiente:

- Hablen acerca del consumo de tabaco y alcohol en su comunidad.
- Elógielo cuando se mantenga firme en contra de la presión negativa de los amigos.
- Explíquele quiénes son sus autoridades.

Actividad familiar

Junto con su hijo(a), investiguen sobre los programas locales que están disponibles para ayudar a las personas a dejar el alcohol y apoyar a sus familias. Dichos programas incluyen Alcohólicos Anónimos, *Al-Anon* e Hijos de alcohólicos (*Adult Children of Alcoholics*). Busquen los números de estas y otras entidades en un directorio telefónico o en los periódicos, o llamen a un hospital local. Ayude a su hijo(a) a organizar la información que encuentren, en la tabla de abajo.

Grupos locales de ayuda

Nombre	Lugar donde está	Día y hora de reuniones	Teléfono

© Harcourt

Name _____ Date _____

School-Home Connection

A Note to Family Members

What We Are Learning About Health

In Chapter 10 of *Harcourt Health and Fitness,* we are learning about

- establishing a healthy self-concept through positive thinking and goal setting.
- ways to form and maintain friendships through effective and positive expression of feelings.
- managing stress at school and in dealing with new situations.
- respecting and understanding people's differences.

 Visit **www.harcourtschool.com/health** for links to parent resources.

How You Can Help

Parental involvement in the school environment is part of a coordinated school health plan that includes the home, school, community, and social services. You can support your school through increased communication and by volunteering your time or talents. At home you can support your child's learning by

- helping your child maintain a good self-image and attitude.
- discussing situations in which stress management could be practiced.
- praising your child when he or she accepts and respects differences in others.

A Family Activity

Resolving conflicts takes practice. Work together to fill in the table below. Have your child describe one or more minor conflicts or disagreements that he or she has seen at school. For each conflict, write down how the people behaved. Did they fight physically? Did they argue with words? Was the conflict resolved? Were there better ways to handle some of the conflicts? List these more positive behaviors, and talk about ways to use these behaviors when involved in conflicts.

Resolving Conflicts

Description of Conflict	Description of Behavior	Better Ways to Handle Conflict

La escuela y la casa

Nota para los familiares

Lo que estamos aprendiendo acerca de la Salud

En el Capítulo 10 de *Harcourt Health and Fitness* estamos aprendiendo acerca de:

- Cómo adquirir una autoimagen sana por medio de la actitud positiva y el establecimiento de metas adecuadas.
- Las maneras de ganar y conservar amistades por medio de la expresión positiva y efectiva de los sentimientos.
- Cómo manejar el estrés y las situaciones nuevas en la escuela.
- La importancia de respetar y entender las diferencias en las personas.

 Visite **www.harcourtschool.com/health** para encontrar enlaces con recursos en inglés para los padres.

Cómo puede usted ayudar

La participación familiar en las actividades escolares forma parte de un plan de salud organizado que incluye la casa, la escuela, la comunidad y los servicios sociales. Usted puede apoyar a la escuela manteniendo una buena comunicación y ofreciendo su tiempo y sus talentos como voluntario. En casa, usted puede apoyar el aprendizaje de su hijo(a) haciendo lo siguiente:

- Ayúdelo a conservar una autoimagen y una actitud positivas.
- Hablen sobre las situaciones que requieren un manejo adecuado del estrés.
- Elógielo cuando acepta y respeta las diferencias en otras pesonas.

Actividad familiar

La resolución de problemas requiere práctica. Pida a su hijo(a) que describa algunas situaciones en las que tuvo que enfrentar desacuerdos o conflictos menores en la escuela, en la tabla de abajo. Pídale que escriba cómo se comportaron las personas involucradas. ¿Hubo pelea? ¿Discutieron? ¿Cómo se resolvió el conflicto? ¿Se podría haber resuelto de otra forma? ¿Como cuál? Hablen de las acciones positivas y de cómo usarlas para resolver conflictos.

Formas de resolver conflictos

Descripción del conflicto	Qué pasó	Cómo resolverlo mejor

© Harcourt

School-Home Connection

A Note to Family Members

What We Are Learning About Health

In Chapter 11 of *Harcourt Health and Fitness,* we are learning about

- how family members support each other during times of change.
- working together with family to find out health information and advice.
- recognizing communication needs within a family.
- supporting family members in new situations.

 Visit **www.harcourtschool.com/health** for links to parent resources.

How You Can Help

Parental involvement in the school environment is part of a coordinated school health plan that includes the home, school, community, and social services. You can support your school through increased communication and by volunteering your time or talents. At home you can support your child's learning by

- discussing more mature responsibilities as your child grows older.
- helping your child develop an exercise plan for the family.
- praising your child's efforts to recognize when support for a family member is needed.

A Family Activity

Family change can come to families suddenly or gradually. These can be stressful times for a child and his or her family. After your child has reviewed the chapter, have him or her fill out the table below. Discuss any of the changes that have happened to your family or to families in your neighborhood.

Dealing with Change in Families

Change	Common Effects	Dealing with the Change
Remarriage		
Birth of a baby		
Moving		
Death		

La escuela y la casa

Nota para los familiares

Lo que estamos aprendiendo acerca de la Salud

En el Capítulo 11 de *Harcourt Health and Fitness* estamos aprendiendo acerca de:

• Las diferentes maneras en que los familiares se ayudan unos a otros cuando ocurren cambios.

• El trabajo en familia para aprender más sobre temas de salud y cómo dar y recibir consejos.

• Formas de reconocer las necesidades de comunicación dentro de la familia.

• Cómo ayudar a un familiar cuando está pasando por una experiencia totalmente nueva.

 Visite **www.harcourtschool.com/health** para encontrar enlaces con recursos en inglés para los padres.

Cómo puede usted ayudar

La participación familiar en las actividades escolares forma parte de un plan de salud organizado que incluye la casa, la escuela, la comunidad y los servicios sociales. Usted puede apoyar a la escuela manteniendo una buena comunicación y ofreciendo su tiempo y sus talentos como voluntario. En casa, usted puede apoyar el aprendizaje de su hijo(a) haciendo lo siguiente:

• Hablen acerca de las nuevas responsabilidades que su hijo(a) adquiere a medida que crece.

• Ayúdelo a crear un plan de ejercicios para toda la familia.

• Elógielo cuando vea que se esfuerza por ayudar a otro familiar.

Actividad familiar

Hay cambios que ocurren paulatinamente y hay otros que ocurren de un momento a otro. Como quiera que sea, todo cambio puede producir estrés tanto en el niño como en toda la familia. Pida a su hijo(a) que repase el contenido del capítulo y luego llene la tabla de abajo. Hablen sobre los cambios que su familia u otras familias de su barrio han experimentado.

Cómo sobrellevar los cambios

Cambios ocurridos	Consecuencias	Maneras de sobrellevarlos
Un nuevo matrimonio		
Un bebé		
Una nueva casa		
Una muerte		

© Harcourt

School-Home Connection

What We Are Learning About Health

In Chapter 12 of *Harcourt Health and Fitness,* we are learning about

- how government and private agencies serve public health.
- the role of health organizations in community health, from disease control and prevention to pollution control.
- setting goals to promote a healthful community and environment.
- being a good citizen by taking pride in the community.

 Visit **www.harcourtschool.com/health** for links to parent resources.

How You Can Help

Parental involvement in the school environment is part of a coordinated school health plan that includes the home, school, community, and social services. You can support your school through increased communication and by volunteering your time or talents. At home you can support your child's learning by

- discussing how your family has been positively affected by a community health agency.
- helping your child with the three *r*'s around the home: reuse, recycle, and reduce.
- praising your child's efforts to promote the health of the community.

A Family Activity

Most phone directories include a section that lists the names and phone numbers of community service groups. Use the information you find there to make a chart listing three or four service groups in the community or state. Possibilities include the Better Business Bureau and consumer product and safety organizations. Talk about what each group does and why a person might need to call each group.

Service Groups in Your Community

Name of Group	What It Does	Phone Number

La escuela y la casa

Nota para los familiares

Lo que estamos aprendiendo acerca de la Salud

En el Capítulo 12 de *Harcourt Health and Fitness* estamos aprendiendo acerca de:

- Las agencias privadas y del gobierno que trabajan por la salud pública.
- Las funciones de las organizaciones de salud dentro de la comunidad, que incluyen la prevención y el control de las enfermedades y el control de la contaminación.
- Cómo establecer metas para mantener la salubridad de la comunidad y del medio ambiente.
- Cómo ser un buen ciudadano y estar orgulloso de su comunidad.

 Visite **www.harcourtschool.com/health** para encontrar enlaces con recursos en inglés para los padres.

Cómo puede usted ayudar

La participación familiar en las actividades escolares forma parte de un plan de salud organizado que incluye la casa, la escuela, la comunidad y los servicios sociales. Usted puede apoyar a la escuela manteniendo una buena comunicación y ofreciendo su tiempo y sus talentos como voluntario. En casa, usted puede apoyar el aprendizaje de su hijo(a) haciendo lo siguiente:

- Hablen de las experiencias positivas que hayan tenido con una agencia de salud de la comunidad.
- Ayúdelo a practicar los tres pasos de reciclaje en el hogar: volver a usar, reducir y reciclar.
- Elógielo cuando vea que su hijo(a) se esfuerza por ayudar a promover la salud de la comunidad.

Actividad familiar

Llenen la tabla de abajo con el nombre, el número de teléfono y la función de algunos grupos de servicio locales o estatales, como la procuraduría del consumidor (Better Business Bureau) u otras organizaciones de ayuda a los consumidores. En su directorio telefónico local aparece una sección con la información sobre grupos de servicio comunitario. Hablen sobre la función de cada grupo y por qué las personas los necesitan..

Grupos de servicio de la comunidad

Nombre del grupo	Función	Teléfono

Writing Models

The writing models on the following pages are examples of writing for different purposes. Students can consult these models as they work on the writing assignments in the Lesson Summary and Reviews in *Harcourt Health and Fitness.* You may wish to distribute copies of the writing models for students to keep.

You will also find rubrics to use for scoring writing assignments. There are rubrics for Ideas/Content, Organization, Sentence Fluency, Word Choice, Conventions, and Voice.

© Harcourt

Model: Business Letter

In a **business letter**, the writer may request information or express an opinion. A business letter has the same parts as a friendly letter, plus an inside address. This is the receiver's address. A business letter uses a colon after the words in the greeting, and the paragraphs are not indented.

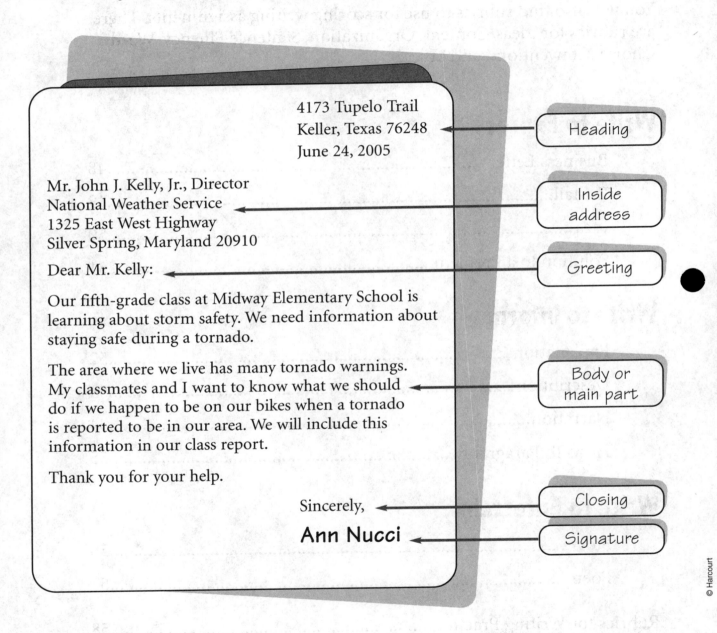

4173 Tupelo Trail
Keller, Texas 76248
June 24, 2005

Heading

Mr. John J. Kelly, Jr., Director
National Weather Service
1325 East West Highway
Silver Spring, Maryland 20910

Inside address

Dear Mr. Kelly:

Greeting

Our fifth-grade class at Midway Elementary School is learning about storm safety. We need information about staying safe during a tornado.

The area where we live has many tornado warnings. My classmates and I want to know what we should do if we happen to be on our bikes when a tornado is reported to be in our area. We will include this information in our class report.

Thank you for your help.

Body or main part

Sincerely,

Closing

Ann Nucci

Signature

Model: E-Mail

Sending **e-mail** is much like sending a letter. However, because it is being sent over a computer, it should be short and to the point. You may wish to include a greeting and signature unless you are sure the receiver recognizes your e-mail address. Include a subject line to describe the content of your e-mail.

Describe the subject of the message on the subject line. The computer automatically puts in the date.

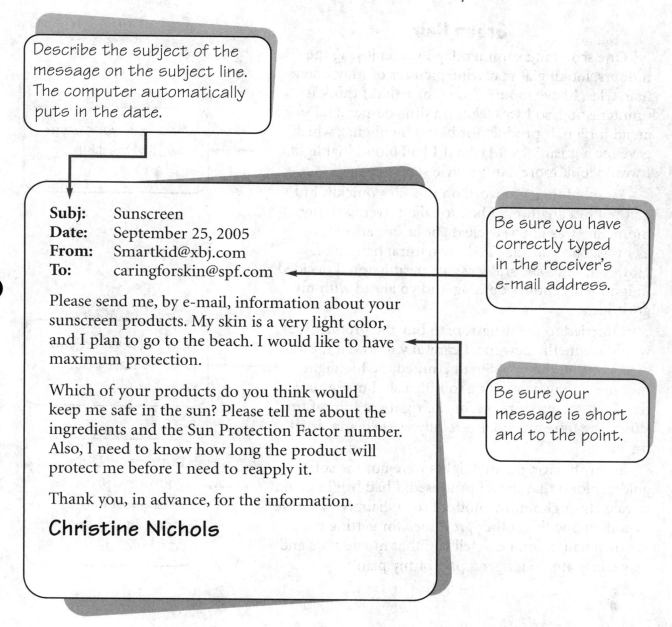

Subj:	Sunscreen
Date:	September 25, 2005
From:	Smartkid@xbj.com
To:	caringforskin@spf.com

Please send me, by e-mail, information about your sunscreen products. My skin is a very light color, and I plan to go to the beach. I would like to have maximum protection.

Which of your products do you think would keep me safe in the sun? Please tell me about the ingredients and the Sun Protection Factor number. Also, I need to know how long the product will protect me before I need to reapply it.

Thank you, in advance, for the information.

Christine Nichols

Be sure you have correctly typed in the receiver's e-mail address.

Be sure your message is short and to the point.

Writing in Health

Model: Idea

An **idea** is a thought about something that you would like to make or do. Choose an idea you had, and tell how that idea came into your mind. Write the steps that were needed to carry out your idea. Tell whether your idea was a success.

Green Hair

One scorching summer day I was enjoying the cool indoors, looking at magazine pictures of movie stars' hairstyles. I have mousy brown hair that I think is uninteresting, so I was feeling a little desperate. I saw an ad for a hair product for blond highlights, which gave me a great idea. Maybe if I had blond highlights, I would look more like a movie star.

> What was your idea? How did you think of it?

I wanted to get to work on this idea quickly, but before I did anything, I had to talk it over with my mom. She was not as excited about this adventure as I was. She said she liked my natural hair color. However, since she still gave me permission, I decided to ignore my mom's opinion and go ahead with my great idea.

I hurried to the drugstore to buy the product that would create the new me. I carefully followed the directions on the box. First I painted the highlight mixture on my hair with a toothbrush. I made sure that I left the mixture on for the right amount of time. When the time was up, I carefully washed and dried my hair.

> What steps did you take to carry out your idea?

To my horror, the highlights were not the soft, golden blond that the ad promised. I had bright green streaks throughout my mousy brown hair. Now I have to come up with another great idea for getting back my own hair color. I can tell you that movie stars and magazines are no longer a part of my plan!

> Elaborate. Did your idea prove to be a good one? How did you feel at the end?

© Harcourt

Writing Model

Writing in Health

Model: Solution to a Problem

You develop a **solution to a problem** by thinking of ways to solve the problem. Explain what advantages and disadvantages you explored before you decided on a particular solution. Finally, tell how well the solution you chose worked.

To Ride or Not to Ride

One day after school, my friends and I decided to go for a bike ride down to the creek, where none of us was permitted to go. After we had been there for a while, Steven suggested that we follow the creek on foot to see where it went. I reminded my friends that it would be getting dark soon, but they said not to worry about it.

An hour later, it was almost sunset, and we were still walking away from where we had parked our bikes. "That's it!" I said. "We need to start riding home before it gets too dark. The light on my bike doesn't work."

"We can't ride our bikes home now!" Jason said. "It's dangerous to ride at night even when you do have a light."

> What was the problem?

"I don't have my reflectors," said Paul. "I was going to buy some new ones, but I completely forgot about it. We'll have a hard time seeing and being seen."

I tried to think of an alternative plan. If we called home and asked for a ride, we would all get into trouble for being at the creek.

> Tell what advantages and disadvantages you weighed to find a solution.

"I know we're going to get into trouble for coming here," I said, "but I'd much rather get into trouble than get run over because a car couldn't see me on my bike in the dark."

I called my mom and told her what had happened, assuming I would be getting the scolding of a lifetime. "You did the right thing, Nick," she said. "You shouldn't have gone there, but I'm proud of you for calling me instead of making that dangerous ride home."

We all got into trouble, but we had made the right choice by calling for help.

> Tell how well the solution worked.

© Harcourt

Writing in Health

Model: Explanation

In an **explanation**, the writer helps the reader understand something. Use exact words to explain what something is, how something works, what happens during a process, or why something happens. Do not include your personal viewpoint in an explanation.

How to Prepare Food Safely

You may have had the unpleasant experience of food poisoning, or maybe you have heard of an outbreak of food poisoning at a local restaurant. Preparing food safely is serious business. Failure to do so could result in someone becoming sick.

> Include a topic sentence.

It is very important to wash your hands with warm, soapy water before you prepare food. If the meat you are about to cook is frozen, do not thaw it on the counter. Germs will grow quickly on the parts of the meat that thaw first and become warmer. Thaw foods in the microwave or in the refrigerator.

> Give a detailed explanation.

After you have finished using a cutting board, clean it with warm, soapy water to remove any juices. It is important to keep the juices of meat, poultry, and fish away from other foods.

If food is undercooked, bacteria might still be present. These bacteria could make you sick. Cook red meat to a temperature of 160°F. Use a meat thermometer to make sure that poultry cooks to a temperature of 180°F. If you want to make sure that fish is cooked thoroughly, test it with a fork to see if it flakes.

> Use exact words.

It is always tempting to sneak a piece of cookie dough before it is baked. However, the uncooked eggs in the cookie dough could make you sick. Do not eat foods that contain uncooked eggs.

It takes a little extra care to prepare food safely, but the result could be healthy eaters coming back for seconds!

© Harcourt

Writing Model

Writing in Health

Model: Description

A **description** uses sensory details to tell about a subject. Use figurative language and imagery to help the reader create a mental picture. You may also tell the reader how you feel by giving your personal viewpoint.

A Puff of Smoke

I love my father very much, but his addiction to cigarettes scares me.

Every morning I listen to my alarm clock's muffled ring, drowned out by my father's rasping cough. I hear him fighting to clear the phlegm out of his oxygen-deprived lungs. His cough is as deep as a crater.

I listen to him turn off the house alarm and unlock the back door. He walks into the crisp morning air to pollute it with his morning smoke. He tips his ashes into the overflowing ashtray that he uses outdoors. The blackened rainwater floods the ashtray like a polluted river. On its side it reads, "Barry's Butts."

I hear the door open and close again. Dad comes into my room to make sure I am awake. When he leans over me, I see a smile that would light a city if not for the yellow tinge of nicotine. The stale smoke on his bathrobe penetrates my nasal passages. I hug my father and rustle myself out of bed.

My mom is preparing a healthful breakfast for my sister and me. Dad never *eats* with us. His cigarette takes the place of breakfast. He sits at the table, holding the newspaper with fingers that are stained yellow from cigarettes. My mom chuckles and tells him that he needs to find a different shirt to wear this morning. There is a small hole on the front of his shirt. Flicked cigarette ashes are responsible. Exasperated, my father goes back to the bedroom, clearing his throat once more.

My father tells me to get my backpack ready because we will be leaving after he has one more cigarette. I nod dutifully, wishing Dad would recognize the concern on my face and have the strength to kick the habit.

> Describe your topic in a main idea sentence.

> Use figurative language.

> Use imagery.

> Express your personal viewpoint.

Writing Model

Writing in Health

Model: Narration

A **personal narrative** is a story about the writer's own experiences. The writer often tells about a lesson he or she learned or a significant event that helped him or her understand something differently.

Healthy Me

If I were to tell about myself, one thing I would say is that I have been best friends with Patty Kelly since second grade. We have a lot in common. Among other things, we both think of ourselves as cool. However, there is one big difference between us: Patty is pretty slim and I am not so slim. I would like to know how to look more like Patty.

> Introduce yourself.

Sometimes Patty and I go to the grocery store with her mom, where she buys each of us an apple to eat on the ride home. My mom says that fruit is too expensive for us to have every day.

When I spend the night at Patty's, we sit down for a big breakfast the next morning. Now that I am learning more about nutrition, I see that a breakfast of oatmeal, juice, and a piece of fruit is a great way to start the day. At my house, we usually have sugary cereal.

> Describe the event that caused you to change.

At Patty's house, we always drink ice water with a slice of lemon. It tastes so refreshing! Patty says that she never eats junk food because she is too full. After dinner, Patty's family goes for a walk with their dog, Skipper. In the evening at my house, my family has a big bowl of popcorn with butter on it as we sit and watch TV.

Patty's mom is a nurse. She says that exercising regularly and eating right are choices we make for a healthy life. I now eat only small amounts of foods that are high in fat or sugar. I make sure I do some kind of physical activity for at least thirty minutes a day. I have lots of energy when I get out of bed to have my healthful breakfast. My family is learning more healthful habits from me, and I'm looking forward to becoming more fit.

> Tell how the event changed you.

Writing Model

Writing in Health

Model: How-To Paragraph

In a **how-to paragraph**, a writer gives steps to tell how to make or do something. List all the materials you will need for the activity. Write the steps in the correct order.

Grandma Minnie's Pasta Sauce

We all know that having a healthful diet means eating plenty of vegetables. One easy way to sneak those vegetables into a meal is to add them to pasta sauce. This favorite family recipe is just the answer. To start, you will need to gather the following ingredients: one 32-ounce can of tomato sauce, one 32-ounce can of whole tomatoes, one-half of a green pepper, one-quarter of an onion, $\frac{1}{4}$ cup grated cheese, two cloves of garlic, and small amounts of basil, parsley, and pepper. To combine the ingredients, you will need a blender, a large pot, and a wooden spoon for stirring.

First, add the tomato sauce to the pot. Next, use the blender to chop and mix the whole tomatoes, green pepper, onion, and garlic. Add this mixture to the pot. Then, add the grated cheese and spices to taste. Finally, cook on medium heat for $\frac{1}{2}$ hour. Pour the hot sauce over your pasta!

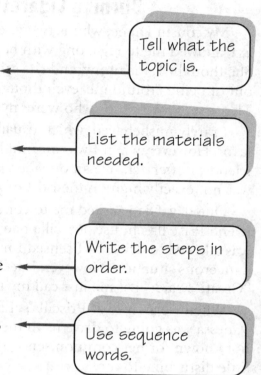

Tell what the topic is.

List the materials needed.

Write the steps in order.

Use sequence words.

Writing Model

Writing in Health

Model: Story

A **story** is writing that includes characters, a setting, and a plot. The characters in a story can be real or imaginary. The main character in a story has a problem to solve. Tell the events of the story in the order in which they happen.

Burning Cigarettes

My cousin Diane, who is two years older than I am, allowed me to tag along with her and her friends. She thought I was funny, and she said she got a kick out of being around me, even though I was younger. That made my friends who were my age think I was cool.

I rarely misbehaved, which usually worked in my favor. However, when I was around Diane and her friends, I often felt like an outsider. Obeying parents was not exactly high on their list of priorities.

One day, Diane asked me to come with her to her friend Priscilla's house. Priscilla had a sister, Vanessa, who was allowed to drive, so I sensed I might be getting into a dangerous situation. However, I decided to go anyway. "Great," I said. "Let me just call my mom and tell her."

When we arrived at Priscilla's, I found out that Vanessa was going to drive us to the mall. Vanessa was not known for her common sense, so this news was a little disturbing to me.

As soon as we got into the car, all the girls decided to light cigarettes. My heart was pounding wildly. I didn't know how to smoke, and I didn't want to smoke. Why hadn't I just gone home when I'd had the chance? My mom would have been furious if she had known I was here. Everyone was looking at me. It was my turn to light a cigarette. Diane started to chuckle. "Just burn the end," she said, "and take a drag." I wondered what she meant by a *drag* but didn't dare ask.

Suddenly, I felt a jolt. Vanessa had plowed into the back of a minivan. The police arrived just after the girls frantically threw away their cigarettes. Vanessa was about to earn her third traffic ticket in six months for this crash.

The car wasn't too banged up. "Do you want me to drive you home?" asked Vanessa.

"No, thanks," I said. Somehow, a safe ride home with my mom sounded much better than being cool.

> Use elaboration to give details about the characters.

> Use exact words to tell about the problem that the character has to solve.

> Give the events of the story in time order.

© Harcourt

Writing Model

Writing in Health

Model: Poem

A **poem** is a way for the writer to describe something or express feelings about a subject. Word choice is important, because it helps create rhythm and rhyme. Poems often use figures of speech, such as similes and metaphors, to help "paint a word picture" for the reader.

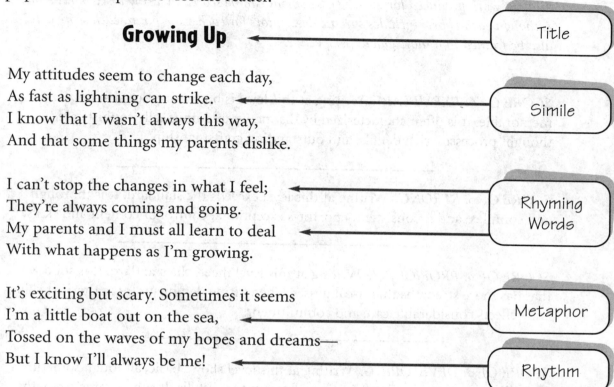

Growing Up ← Title

My attitudes seem to change each day,
As fast as lightning can strike. ← Simile
I know that I wasn't always this way,
And that some things my parents dislike.

I can't stop the changes in what I feel;
They're always coming and going.
My parents and I must all learn to deal ← Rhyming Words
With what happens as I'm growing.

It's exciting but scary. Sometimes it seems
I'm a little boat out on the sea, ← Metaphor
Tossed on the waves of my hopes and dreams—
But I know I'll always be me! ← Rhythm

Rubrics for Writing Practice

A Six-Point Scoring Scale

Student work produced for writing assessment can be scored by using a six-point scale. Although each rubric includes specific descriptors for each score point, each score can also be framed in a more global perspective.

SCORE OF 6: EXEMPLARY. Writing at this level is both exceptional and memorable. It is often characterized by distinctive and unusually sophisticated thought processes, rich details, and outstanding craftsmanship.

SCORE OF 5: STRONG. Writing at this level exceeds the standard. It is thorough and complex, and it consistently portrays exceptional control of content and skills.

SCORE OF 4: PROFICIENT. Writing at this level meets the standard. It is solid work that has more strengths than weaknesses. The writing demonstrates mastery of skills and reflects considerable care and commitment.

SCORE OF 3: DEVELOPING. Writing at this level shows basic, although sometimes inconsistent, mastery and application of content and skills. It shows some strengths but tends to have more weaknesses overall.

SCORE OF 2: EMERGING. Writing at this level is often superficial, fragmented, or incomplete. It may show a partial mastery of content and skills, but it needs considerable development before reflecting the proficient level of performance.

SCORE OF 1: BEGINNING. Writing at this level is minimal. It typically lacks understanding and use of appropriate skills and strategies. The writing may contain major errors.

Rubric for Ideas/Content

Score	Description
6	The writing is exceptionally clear, focused, and interesting. It holds the reader's attention throughout. Main ideas stand out and are developed by strong support and rich details suitable to the audience and the purpose.
5	The writing is clear, focused, and interesting. It holds the reader's attention. Main ideas stand out and are developed by supporting details suitable to the audience and the purpose.
4	The writing is clear and focused. The reader can easily understand the main ideas. Support is present, although it may be limited or rather general.
3	The reader can understand the main ideas, although they may be overly broad or simplistic, and the results may not be effective. Supporting details are often limited, insubstantial, overly general, or occasionally slightly off topic.
2	The main ideas and purpose are somewhat unclear, or development is attempted but minimal.
1	The writing lacks a central idea or purpose.

Rubric for Organization

Score	Description
6	The organization enhances the central idea(s) and its development. The order and structure are compelling and move the reader through the text easily.
5	The organization enhances the central idea(s) and its development. The order and structure are strong and move the reader through the text.
4	The organization is clear and coherent. Order and structure are present but may seem formulaic.
3	An attempt has been made to organize the writing; however, the overall structure is inconsistent or skeletal.
2	The writing lacks a clear organizational structure. An occasional organizational device is discernible; however, either the writing is difficult to follow and the reader has to reread substantial portions, or the piece is simply too short to demonstrate organizational skills.
1	The writing lacks coherence; organization seems haphazard and disjointed. Even after rereading, the reader remains confused.

Rubric for Sentence Fluency

Score	Description
6	The writing has an effective flow and rhythm. Sentences show a high degree of craftsmanship, with consistently strong and varied structure that makes expressive oral reading easy and enjoyable.
5	The writing has an easy flow and rhythm. Sentences are carefully crafted, with strong and varied structure that makes expressive oral reading easy and enjoyable.
4	The writing flows; however, connections between phrases or sentences may be less than fluid. Sentence patterns are somewhat varied, contributing to ease in oral reading.
3	The writing tends to be mechanical rather than fluid. Occasional awkward constructions may force the reader to slow down or reread.
2	The writing tends to be either choppy or rambling. Awkward constructions often force the reader to slow down or reread.
1	The writing is difficult to follow or to read aloud. Sentences tend to be incomplete, rambling, or very awkward.

Rubric for Word Choice

Score	Description
6	The words convey the intended message in an exceptionally interesting, precise, and natural way appropriate to the audience and the purpose. The writer employs a rich, broad range of words that have been carefully chosen and thoughtfully placed for impact.
5	The words convey the intended message in an interesting, precise, and natural way appropriate to the audience and the purpose. The writer employs a broad range of words that have been carefully chosen and thoughtfully placed for impact.
4	The words effectively convey the intended message. The writer employs a variety of words that are functional and appropriate to the audience and the purpose.
3	The language is quite ordinary, lacking interest, precision, and variety, or may be inappropriate to the audience and the purpose in places. The writer does not employ a variety of words, producing a sort of "generic" paper filled with familiar words and phrases.
2	The language is monotonous and/or misused, detracting from the meaning and impact.
1	The writing shows an extremely limited vocabulary or is so filled with misuses of words that the meaning is obscured. Because of vague or imprecise language, only the most general kind of message is communicated.

Rubric for Conventions

Score	Description
6	The writing demonstrates exceptionally strong control of standard writing conventions (e.g., punctuation, spelling, capitalization, paragraph breaks, grammar, and usage) and uses them effectively to enhance communication. Errors are so few and so minor that the reader can easily skim right over them unless specifically searching for them.
5	The writing demonstrates strong control of standard writing conventions (e.g., punctuation, spelling, capitalization, paragraph breaks, grammar, and usage) and uses them effectively to enhance communication. Errors are so few and so minor that they do not impede readability.
4	The writing demonstrates control of standard writing conventions (e.g., punctuation, spelling, capitalization, paragraph breaks, grammar, and usage). Minor errors, while perhaps noticeable, do not impede readability.
3	The writing demonstrates limited control of standard writing conventions (e.g., punctuation, spelling, capitalization, paragraph breaks, grammar, and usage). Errors begin to impede readability.
2	The writing demonstrates little control of standard writing conventions. Frequent, significant errors impede readability.
1	Numerous errors in usage, spelling, capitalization, and punctuation repeatedly distract the reader and make the text difficult to read. In fact, the severity and frequency of errors are so overwhelming that the reader finds it difficult to focus on the message and must reread for meaning.

Rubric for Voice

Score	Description
6	The writer has chosen a voice appropriate for the topic, purpose, and audience. The writer seems deeply committed to the topic, and there is an exceptional sense of "writing to be read." The writing is expressive, engaging, or sincere.
5	The writer has chosen a voice appropriate for the topic, purpose, and audience. The writer seems committed to the topic, and there is a sense of "writing to be read." The writing is expressive, engaging, or sincere.
4	A voice is present. The writer demonstrates commitment to the topic, and there may be a sense of "writing to be read." In places the writing is expressive, engaging, or sincere.
3	The writer's commitment to the topic seems inconsistent. A sense of the writer may emerge at times; however, the voice is either inappropriately personal or inappropriately impersonal.
2	The writing provides little sense of involvement or commitment. There is no evidence that the writer has chosen a suitable voice.
1	The writing seems to lack a sense of involvement or commitment.

Focus Skill

Identify Cause and Effect

Cause:

Effect:

Reading Skill Graphic Organizer

Compare and Contrast

Topic:

Alike

Different

Focus Skill

Draw Conclusions

What I Read		What I Know		Conclusion:

+ =

Focus Skill

Reading Skill Graphic Organizer

Identify Main Idea and Details

Main Idea:

Detail:

Detail:

Detail:

Reading Skill Graphic Organizer

Sequence

1.

↓

2.

↓

3.

Reading Skill Graphic Organizer

Summarize

Focus Skill

Main Idea:

+

Details:

=

Summary:

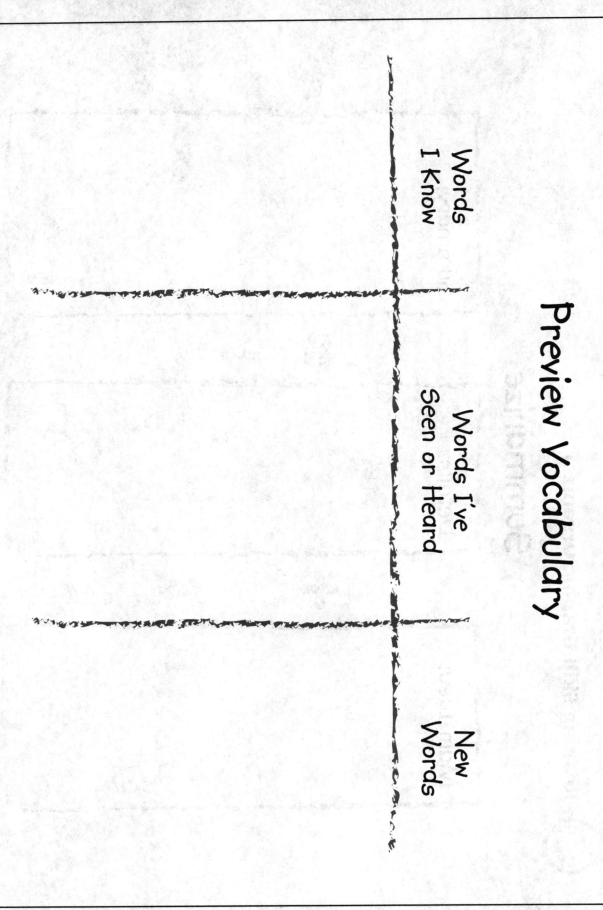

Preview Vocabulary

Words I Know	Words I've Seen or Heard	New Words

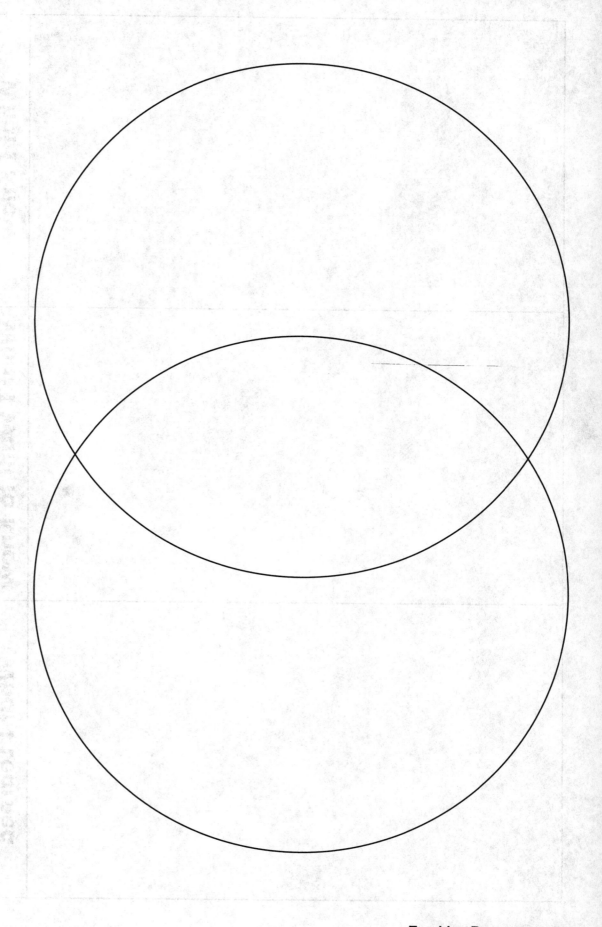

Venn Diagram

K-W-L Chart

What I Know	What I Want to Know	What I Learned

Web

Chart

Knowledge Chart

Topic_____

Prior Knowledge	New Knowledge
1.	1.
2.	2.
3.	3.
4.	4.
5.	5.
6.	6.
7.	7.

Project Plan

What I Want to Find Out

1.

How I Can Find Out

2.

What I Need to Do

3.

Materials

How I Can Share Information

4.

Introduction to the Health and Safety Handbook

Using the Health and Safety Handbook

This section of *Teaching Resources* provides information that addresses important health concerns for students, such as nutrition, physical fitness, safety, and first aid. In addition, it identifies life skills and character traits that are learned early in life and are used in daily interaction with others. This section is intended to supplement and extend the content of the *Student Edition.*

In the Classroom

You can use these pages as stand-alone lessons. You may wish to make copies of these pages for students to compile in a personal health and safety handbook as you teach core lessons from the *Student Edition.*

At Home

You may wish to send copies of these pages home so that students can discuss the tips and topics with their families. The copies can also serve as a reference if students are completing health projects at home.

Health and Safety Handbook
Contents

© Harcourt

Understanding Life Skills

Having good health isn't just knowing the facts about what to eat or how to stay well. It's also thinking critically about those facts and knowing how to apply them to your daily life. Using life skills to apply your growing health knowledge can help you reach the goal of good health.

Communicate

In order to communicate well, you need to explain your ideas, needs, or feelings in a way that others can understand. You also need to listen to and try to understand what others have to say.

Steps for Communicating

1. Understand your audience.
2. Give a clear message.
3. Listen carefully, and answer any questions.
4. Gather feedback.

Ways to Give a Clear Message

- Use "I" messages.
- Use a respectful tone of voice.
- Make eye contact.
- Use appropriate body language.
- Express ideas in a clear, organized way.

Make Responsible Decisions

When you make decisions, you think about a group of choices and decide on the wisest thing to do in order to avoid risky situations or health risks.

Steps for Making Decisions

1. Find out about the choices you could make.
2. Eliminate choices that are illegal or against your family rules.
3. Ask yourself: What is the possible result of each choice? Does the choice show good character?
4. Decide on what seems to be the best choice.

© Harcourt

Understanding Life Skills

Manage Stress

Everyone feels stress. Knowing how to manage your stress can help you get through tense or exciting situations.

Steps for Managing Stress

1. Know what stress feels like and what causes it.

2. Try to determine the cause of the stress.

3. Do something that will help you relieve the feelings of stress.

Ways to Relieve Stress

- Do deep breathing and muscle relaxing exercises.

- Take a walk, exercise, or play a sport.

- Talk to someone you trust about the way you're feeling.

- Watch a funny movie or television show.

- Do something creative such as write, dance, or draw.

Refuse

Knowing what to say *before* you are asked to do something you don't want to do can keep you moving toward good health.

How to Refuse

- Say **no** firmly, and state your reasons for saying **no**.

- Remember a consequence, and keep saying **no**.

- Suggest something else to do.

- Repeat **no**, and walk away. Leave the door open for the other person to join you.

Other Ways to Refuse

- Continue to repeat **no**.

- Change the subject.

- Avoid possible problem situations.

- Ignore the person. Give him or her the "cold shoulder."

- Stay with people who also refuse to do unhealthful actions.

- Reverse the peer pressure.

- Use humor or any other nonviolent way that works.

© Harcourt

Understanding Life Skills

Resolve Conflicts

You must choose and use strategies to communicate and compromise in order to find solutions to problems or to avoid violence.

Steps for Resolving Conflicts

1. Use "I" messages to tell how you feel.

2. Listen to the other person. Consider the other person's point of view.

3. Talk about a solution.

4. Find a way for both sides to win.

Ways to Talk About a Solution

- Negotiate.

- Ask for a mediator.

- Take a break until everyone cools down.

- Make a decision by consensus.

- Use humor if appropriate.

Set Goals

When you set goals, you must decide on a change you want to make and then take actions to make that change happen.

Steps for Setting Goals

1. Choose a goal.

2. Plan steps to meet the goal. Determine whether you will need any help.

3. Check your progress as you work toward the goal.

4. Reflect on and evaluate your progress toward the goal.

© Harcourt

Building Good Character

These are values we choose to help guide us in our daily living. The rules that come from these values are the ground rules of good behavior.

Caring

"It is one of the most beautiful compensations of life, that no man can sincerely try to help another without helping himself."

—Ralph Waldo Emerson

DO
- Support and value family members.
- Be a good friend and share your feelings.
- Show concern for others.
- Thank people who help you.
- Help people in need.

DON'T
- Don't be selfish.
- Don't expect rewards for being caring.
- Don't gossip.
- Don't hurt anyone's feelings.

How do YOU show CARING?

Citizenship

"We must learn to live together as brothers or perish together as fools."

—Martin Luther King, Jr.

DO
- Take pride in your school, community, state, and country.
- Obey laws and rules and respect authority.
- Be a good neighbor.
- Help keep your school and neighborhood safe and clean.
- Cooperate with others.
- Protect the environment.

DON'T
- Don't break rules and laws.
- Don't waste natural resources.
- Don't damage public property or the property of others.
- Don't litter or hurt the environment in other ways.

How do YOU show CITIZENSHIP?

Health and Safety Handbook

Building Good Character

Caring	Citizenship	Fairness	Respect	Responsibility	Trustworthiness

These are values we choose to help guide us in our daily living. The rules that come from these values are the ground rules of good behavior.

Fairness

"Justice cannot be for one side alone, but must be for both."

—**Eleanor Roosevelt**

DO
- Play by the rules.
- Be a good sport.
- Share.
- Take turns.
- Listen to the opinions of others.

DON'T
- Don't take more than your share.
- Don't be a bad loser or a bad winner.
- Don't take advantage of others.
- Don't blame others without cause.
- Don't cut in front of others in line.

How do YOU show FAIRNESS?

Respect

"I believe . . . that every human mind feels pleasure in doing good to another."

—**Thomas Jefferson**

DO
- Treat others the way you want to be treated.
- Accept people who are different from you.
- Be polite and use good manners.
- Be considerate of the feelings of others.
- Stay calm when you are angry.
- Develop self-respect and self-confidence.

DON'T
- Don't use bad language.
- Don't insult or embarrass anyone.
- Don't threaten or bully anyone.
- Don't hit or hurt anyone.

How do YOU show RESPECT?

© Harcourt

Building Good Character

These are values we choose to help guide us in our daily living. The rules that come from these values are the ground rules of good behavior.

Responsibility

"Responsibility is the price of greatness."

—**Winston Churchill**

DO

- Practice self-control and self-discipline.
- Express feelings, needs, and wants in appropriate ways.
- Practice good health habits.
- Keep yourself safe.
- Keep trying. Do your best.
- Complete tasks.
- Set goals and carry them out.
- Be a good role model.

DON'T

- Don't smoke. Don't use alcohol or other drugs.
- Don't do things that are unsafe or destructive.
- Don't be swayed by negative peer pressure.
- Don't deny or make excuses for your mistakes.
- Don't leave your work for others to do.
- Don't lose or misuse your belongings.

How do YOU show RESPONSIBILITY?

Trustworthiness

"What you do speaks so loudly that I cannot hear what you say."

—**Ralph Waldo Emerson**

DO

- Be honest. Tell the truth.
- Do the right thing.
- Report dangerous situations.
- Be dependable.
- Be loyal to your family, friends, and country.
- Take care of things you borrow, and return them promptly.

DON'T

- Don't tell lies.
- Don't cheat.
- Don't steal.
- Don't break promises.
- Don't borrow without asking first.

How do YOU show TRUSTWORTHINESS?

Good Nutrition

MyPyramid

No one food or food group supplies all the nutrients you need. That's why it's important to eat a variety of foods from all the food groups. MyPyramid can help you choose healthful foods in the right amounts. By choosing a good balance of foods from all the groups on the pyramid, you will eat nutrient-rich foods that provide your body with energy to grow and develop.

The number of servings from each food group is suggested for children ages 9–13.

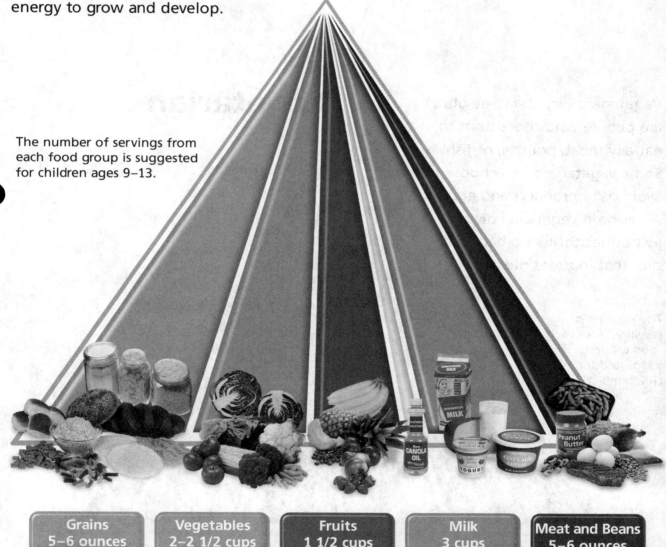

© Harcourt

| Grains 5–6 ounces | Vegetables 2–2 1/2 cups | Fruits 1 1/2 cups | Milk 3 cups | Meat and Beans 5–6 ounces |

Good Nutrition
More Food Guide Pyramids

MyPyramid from the United States Department of Agriculture, or USDA, (page 83) shows common foods from the United States. Foods from different cultures and lifestyles also can make up a healthful diet. The other pyramids shown here can help you to add interesting new foods to your diet.

Vegetarians (vej·uh·TAIR·ee·uhnz) are people who choose not to eat any meat, poultry, or fish. Some vegetarians also choose to avoid dairy products and eggs. A balanced vegetarian diet is just as healthful as a balanced diet that includes meats.

The number of servings from each food group is suggested for children 9–13.

Vegetarian

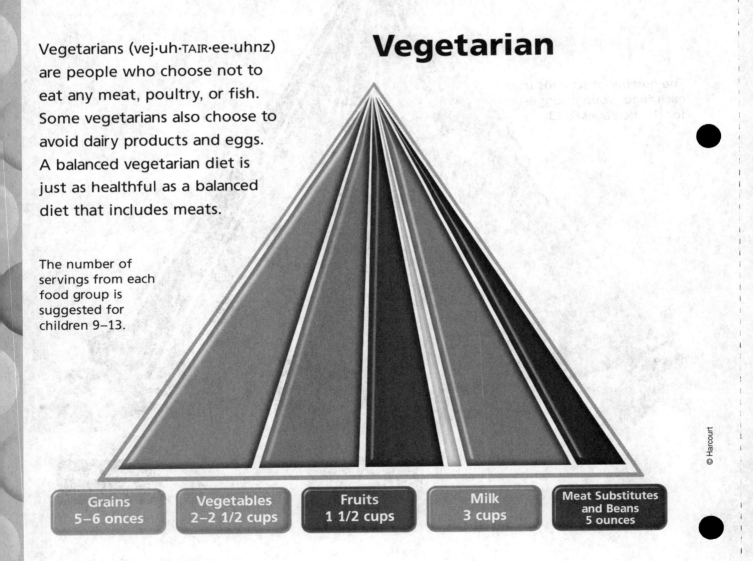

| Grains 5–6 onces | Vegetables 2–2 1/2 cups | Fruits 1 1/2 cups | Milk 3 cups | Meat Substitutes and Beans 5 ounces |

The tops of these two pyramids differ from the one on page 83. They suggest eating seafood, poultry, eggs, and meat each week or month rather than each day. Moderate daily use of vegetable oils is also recommended. What other differences do you notice?

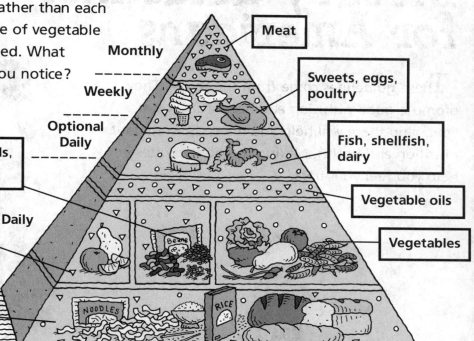

Asian

Monthly

Weekly

Optional Daily

Meat

Sweets, eggs, poultry

Fish, shellfish, dairy

Dried beans, nuts, seeds, meat substitutes

Vegetable oils

Vegetables

Daily

Fruit

Noodles, bread, rice, millets, and other grains

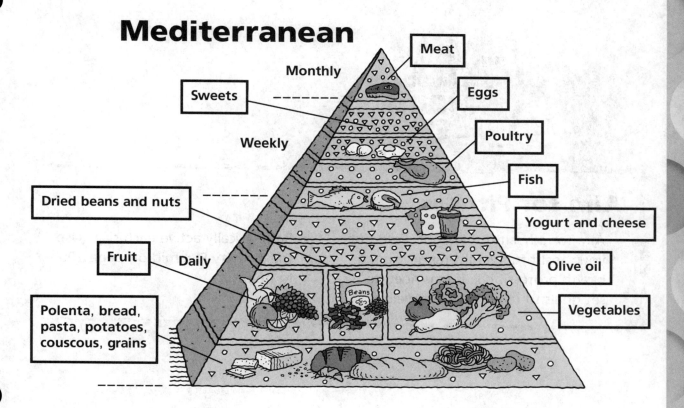

Mediterranean

Monthly

Weekly

Daily

Meat

Sweets

Eggs

Poultry

Fish

Dried beans and nuts

Yogurt and cheese

Fruit

Olive oil

Polenta, bread, pasta, potatoes, couscous, grains

Vegetables

© Harcourt

Good Nutrition

Dietary Guidelines for Americans

These guidelines come from the USDA. They promote good nutrition and healthful choices. Following them will help you make choices about nutrition and health. Making the right choices will help you feel your best.

Aim for Fitness

- Aim for a healthful weight. Find out your healthful weight range from a health professional. If you need to, set goals to reach a better weight.

- Be physically active each day. (Use the Activity Pyramid on page 100 to help you.)

© Harcourt

Build a Healthful Base

- Use MyPyramid to guide your food choices.

- Each day, choose a variety of whole grains, such as wheat, oats and rice.

- Each day, choose a variety of fruits and vegetables.

- Keep food safe to eat. (Follow the tips on pages 89 and 92 for safely preparing and storing food.)

Choose Sensibly

- Choose a diet that is moderate in total fat and low in saturated fat and cholesterol.

- Choose foods and drinks that are low in sugar. Lower the amount of sugar you eat.

- Choose foods that are low in salt. When you prepare foods, use very little salt.

© Harcourt

Good Nutrition

Estimating Amounts

MyPyramid suggests an amount to eat daily from each group. But these amounts aren't necessarily how much you eat at a meal. A plate full of macaroni and cheese may contain $1\frac{1}{2}$ cups of macaroni and 3 ounces of cheese. That's about half your Grains and all your Milk at one sitting! The table below can help you estimate how much you are eating.

Food Group	Common Amount Eaten	Easy Ways to Estimate Amounts
Grains Group	$\frac{1}{2}$ cup cooked pasta, rice, or cereal 1 slice bread, $\frac{1}{2}$ bagel 1 cup ready-to-eat (dry) cereal	• 1 slice of bread or $\frac{1}{2}$ medium bagel is about 1 oz. • 1 oz of cooked rice, oats, or pasta would fill an ice cream scoop. • A fistful of whole-grain cereal flakes is about 1 oz.
Vegetables Group	1 cup raw leafy vegetables $\frac{1}{2}$ cup other vegetables, cooked or chopped raw $\frac{1}{2}$ cup tomato sauce	• A cup of raw vegetables is about the size of a tennis ball. • $\frac{1}{2}$ cup of cooked or chopped vegetables would just about fill an ice-cream scoop.
Fruits Group	1 medium apple, pear, or orange; 1 medium banana; $\frac{1}{2}$ cup chopped or cooked fruit; 1 cup fresh fruit; $\frac{1}{2}$ cup fruit juice	• A medium piece of fruit is about the size of a baseball.
Milk Group	$1\frac{1}{2}$ oz cheese; 1 cup yogurt; 1 cup milk	• A piece of cheese about the size of three dominoes equals the same amount of calcium in a cup of milk.
Meat & Beans Group	2–3 oz lean meat, chicken, or fish 2 tablespoons peanut butter $\frac{1}{2}$ cup cooked dry beans	• An ounce of beans would fill an ice cream scoop. • A 3-oz portion of cooked meat, fish, or poultry is about the size of a computer mouse.
Oils	1 teaspoon canola oil	• 1 teaspoon is about the size of a penny or a fingertip

© Harcourt

Preparing Foods Safely

Fight Bacteria

You probably already know to throw away food that smells bad or looks moldy. But food doesn't have to look or smell bad to make you ill. To keep your food safe and yourself from becoming ill, follow the steps outlined in the picture below. And remember—when in doubt, throw it out!

FIGHT BAC!

Keep Food Safe From Bacteria

CLEAN
Wash hands and surfaces often.

SEPARATE
Don't cross-contaminate.

CHILL
Refrigerate promptly.

COOK
Cook to proper temperatures.

Preparing Foods Safely

Kitchen Safety

Sometimes you may cook a meal or prepare a snack for yourself. Be careful—kitchens can be dangerous. You need to follow safety rules to avoid burns, cuts, and other accidental injuries. You should be especially careful if you're home by yourself.

General Rules

- Follow rules for preparing and storing food safely (page 92).

- Be sure a responsible adult knows what you plan to cook and which kitchen tools you will use.

- Learn fire safety rules for the home.

- To avoid the risk of burns and fires, use the stove and oven as little as possible.

- Clean up after yourself. Turn off all appliances before you leave the kitchen.

Stoves and Ovens

- Get an adult's permission to use the stove or oven. If possible, use a microwave instead.

- Keep clothing away from burners. Avoid clothes with sleeves or laces that hang down; they could catch fire.

- Keep pot handles turned in toward the center of the stove.

- Use an oven mitt to handle hot trays or metal pot handles. A mitt covers your whole hand.

- Be sure you have a firm grip before you lift a container of hot food.

Microwaves

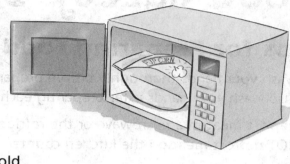

Always follow the directions on the food label. Remember these rules:

- Be careful when you take food out of a microwave. Even if the container isn't hot, steam can burn you.

- Never use metal containers, dishes with gold or silver decoration, or aluminum foil in a microwave. The metal can cause sparks or even start a fire.

- Never use a microwave to heat only water. When heating water, always place a non-metal object such as a wooden stirrer in the container.

Appliances and Kitchen Tools

- Check with an adult to find out which appliances you are allowed to use.

- Never turn an appliance off or on while your hands are wet.

- Kitchen knives are sharp and very dangerous. You should use knives and other sharp kitchen tools only with an adult's permission.

Food Safety Tips

Tips for Preparing Food

- Wash your hands thoroughly before preparing food. Also wash your hands after preparing each dish.

- Defrost meat in a microwave or the refrigerator. Do NOT defrost meat on the kitchen counter.

- Keep raw meat, poultry, and fish and their juices away from other food.

- Wash cutting boards, knives, and countertops immediately after cutting up meat, poultry, or fish. Never use the same cutting board for meats and vegetables without thoroughly washing the board first.

Tips for Cooking Food

- Cook all food thoroughly, especially meat. This will kill bacteria that can make you ill.

- Red meats should be cooked to a temperature of 160°F. Poultry should be cooked to 180°F. When fish is safely cooked, it flakes easily with a fork.

- Eggs should be cooked until the yolks are firm. Never eat foods or drink anything containing raw eggs. Never eat uncooked cookie dough made with raw eggs.

Tips for Cleaning Up the Kitchen

- Wash all dishes, utensils, and countertops with hot, soapy water.

- Store leftovers in small containers that will cool quickly in the refrigerator. Don't leave leftovers on the counter to cool.

- Your refrigerator should be 40°F or colder.

- Write the date on leftovers. Don't store them for more than five days.

Being Physically Active
Guidelines for a Good Workout

There are three things you should do every time you are going to exercise—warm up, work out, and cool down.

Warm Up: When you warm up, your heartbeat rate, respiration rate, and body temperature gradually increase and more blood begins to flow to your muscles. As your body warms up, your flexibility increases, helping you avoid muscle stiffness after exercising. People who warm up are also less likely to have exercise-related injuries. Your warm-up should include five minutes of stretching and five minutes of a low-level form of your workout exercise. For example, if you are going to run for your primary exercise, you should spend five minutes stretching, concentrating on your legs and lower back, and five minutes walking before you start running. Some simple stretches are shown on pages 98–99.

Work Out: The main part of your exercise routine should be an aerobic exercise that lasts twenty to thirty minutes. Some common aerobic exercises include walking, bicycling, jogging, swimming, cross-country skiing, jumping rope, dancing, and playing racket sports. You should choose an activity that is fun for you and that you will enjoy doing over a long period of time. You may want to mix up the types of activities you do. This helps you work different muscle groups and provides a better overall workout. Some common aerobic exercises are shown on pages 94–95.

Cool Down: When you finish your aerobic exercise, you need to give your body time to return to normal. You also need to stretch again. This portion of your workout is called a cool-down. Start your cool-down with three to five minutes of low-level activity. For example, if you have been running, you may want to jog and then walk during this time. Then do stretching exercises to prevent soreness and stiffness.

Being Physically Active

Building a Strong Heart and Lungs

Aerobic activities, those that cause deep breathing and a fast heartbeat rate for at least twenty minutes, help both your heart and your lungs. Because your heart is a muscle, it gets stronger with exercise. A strong heart doesn't have to work as hard to pump blood to the rest of your body. Exercise also allows your lungs to hold more air. With a strong heart and lungs, your cells get oxygen faster and your body works more efficiently.

◄ **Swimming** Swimming may provide the best overall body workout of any sport. It uses all the major muscle groups and improves flexibility. The risk of injury is low, because the water supports your weight, greatly reducing stress on the joints. Just be sure to swim only when a lifeguard is present.

▶ **In-Line Skating** In-line skating gives your heart and lungs a great workout. Remember to always wear a helmet when skating. Always wear protective pads on your elbows and knees, and guards on your wrists, too. Learning how to skate, stop, and fall correctly will reduce your chance of injury.

© Harcourt

Health and Safety Handbook

▶ **Tennis** To get the best aerobic workout from tennis, you should run as fast, far, and hard as you can during the game. Move away from the ball so that you can step into it as you hit it. Finally, try to involve your entire body in every move.

◀ **Walking** A fast-paced walk is a terrific way to build your endurance. The only equipment you need is a good pair of shoes and clothes appropriate for the weather. Walking with a friend can make this exercise a lot of fun.

▶ **Bicycling** Bicycling provides good aerobic activity that places little stress on the joints. It's also a great way to see the countryside. Be sure to use a bike that fits and to learn and follow the rules of the road. And *always* wear your helmet!

Being Physically Active
The President's Challenge

The President's Challenge is a physical fitness program designed for students ages 6 to 17. It's made up of five activities that promote physical fitness. Each participant receives an emblem patch and a certificate signed by the President.

The Five Awards

 Presidential Physical Fitness Award—presented to students scoring in the top 15 percent in all events.

 National Physical Fitness Award—presented to students scoring in the top 50 percent in all events.

 Health Fitness Award—awarded to all other participants.

 Participant Physical Fitness Award—presented to students who complete all items but score below the top 50 percent in one or more items.

 Active Lifestyle Award—recognizes students who participate in daily physical activity of any type for five days per week, 60 minutes a day, or 11,000 pedometer steps for six weeks.

The five activities

1. **Curl-Ups or Sit-Ups** measure abdominal muscle strength.

   - Lie on the floor with your arms across your chest and your legs bent. Have a partner hold your feet.

   - Lift your upper body off the ground, and then lower it until it just touches the floor.

   - Repeat as many times as you can in one minute.

2. **Shuttle Run** measures leg strength and endurance.

   - Run to the blocks and pick one up.

   - Bring it back to the starting line.

   - Repeat with the other block.

© Harcourt

3. One-Mile Run or Walk measures leg muscle strength and heart and lung endurance.

- Run or walk a mile as fast as you can.

4. Pull-Ups measure the strength and endurance of arm and shoulder muscles.

- Hang by your hands from a bar.

- Pull your body up until your chin is over the bar. Lower your body again without touching the floor.

- Repeat as many times as you can.

5. V-Sit Reach measures the flexibility of your legs and back.

- Sit on the floor with your feet behind the line.

- Reach forward as far as you can.

© Harcourt

Health and Safety Handbook

Teaching Resources • 97

Being Physically Active

Warm-Up and Cool-Down Stretches

Before you exercise, you should always warm up your muscles. The warm-up stretches shown here should be held for at least fifteen to twenty seconds and repeated at least three times. At the end of your workout, spend about two minutes repeating some of these stretches.

▲ **Hurdler's Stretch** HINT—Keep the toes of your extended leg pointed up.

◄ **Thigh Stretch** HINT—Keep both hands flat on the floor. Try to lean as far forward as you can.

► **Upper-Back and Shoulder Stretch** HINT—Try to stretch your hand down so that it lies flat against your back.

© Harcourt

▼ **Sit-and-Reach Stretch**
HINT—Remember to bend at the waist. Keep your eyes on your toes!

▼ **Shoulder and Chest Stretch** HINT—Pulling your hands slowly toward the floor makes this stretch more effective. Keep your elbows straight, but not locked!

▲ **Calf Stretch** HINT—Remember to keep both feet on the floor during this stretch. Try changing the distance between your feet. Is the stretch better for you when your legs are closer together or farther apart?

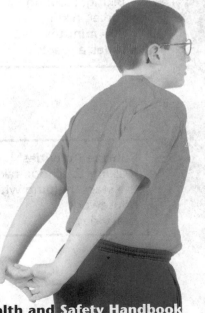

Tips for Stretching

• Never bounce when stretching.

• Remember to hold each stretch for fifteen to twenty seconds.

• Breathe normally. This helps your body get the oxygen it needs.

• Stretch only until you feel a slight pull, NOT until it hurts.

© Harcourt

Health and Safety Handbook

Being Physically Active

Planning Your Weekly Activities

Being active every day is important for your overall health. Physical activity strengthens your body systems and helps you manage stress and maintain a healthful weight. The Activity Pyramid, like the Food Guide Pyramid, can help you make a variety of choices in the right amounts to keep your body strong and healthy.

The Activity Pyramid

Sitting Still
Watching television, playing computer games
Small amounts of time

Light Exercise
Playtime, yardwork, softball
2–3 times a week

Strength and Flexibility Exercises
Weight training, dancing, pull-ups
2–3 times a week

Aerobic Exercises
Biking, running, soccer, hiking
30+ minutes, 2–3 times a week

Routine Activities
Walking to school, taking the stairs, helping with housework
Every day

First Aid
For Bleeding-Universal Precautions

You can get some diseases from a person's blood. Avoid touching anyone's blood. Wear protective gloves if possible. To treat an injury, follow the steps.

If someone else is bleeding

1 Wash your hands with soap if possible.

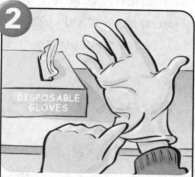

2 Put on protective gloves, if available.

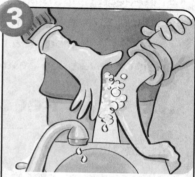

3 Wash small wounds with soap and water. Do not wash serious wounds.

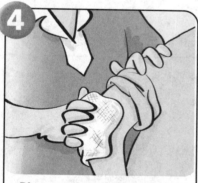

4 Place a clean gauze pad or cloth over the wound. Press firmly for ten minutes. Don't lift the gauze during this time.

5 If you don't have gloves, have the injured person hold the gauze or cloth in place with his or her hand for ten minutes.

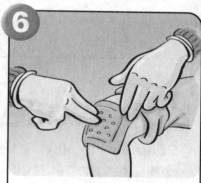

6 If after ten minutes the bleeding has stopped, bandage the wound. If the bleeding has not stopped, continue pressing on the wound and get help.

If you are bleeding

Follow the steps above. You do not need to avoid touching your own blood.

First Aid

For Burns

- Minor burns are called first-degree burns and involve only the top layer of skin. The skin is red and dry, and the burn is painful.

- Second-degree burns cause deeper damage. The burns cause blisters, redness, swelling, and pain.

- Third-degree burns are the most serious because they damage all layers of the skin. The skin is usually white or charred black. The area may feel numb because the nerve endings have been destroyed.

All burns need immediate first aid.

Minor Burns

- Run cool water over the burn or soak it for at least five minutes.

- Cover the burn with a clean, dry bandage.

- Do not put lotion or ointment on the burn.

More Serious Burns

- Cover the burn with a cool, wet bandage or cloth. Do not break any blisters.

- Do not put lotion or ointment on the burn.

- Get help from an adult right away.

For Nosebleeds

- Sit down, and tilt your head forward. Pinch your nostrils together for at least ten minutes.

- You can also put a cloth-covered cold pack on the bridge of your nose.

- If your nose continues to bleed, get help from an adult.

© Harcourt

First Aid
For Choking

If someone else is choking

1 Recognize the Universal Choking Sign—grasping the throat with both hands. This sign means a person is choking and needs help.

2 Stand behind the person, and put your arms around his or her waist. Place your fist above the person's belly button.

3 Grab your fist with your other hand. Pull your hands toward yourself, and give five quick, hard, upward thrusts on the person's stomach.

If you are choking when alone

1 Make a fist, and place it above your belly button. Grab your fist with your other hand. Pull your hands up with a quick, hard thrust.

2 Or keep your hands on your belly, lean your body over the back of a chair or over a counter, and shove your fist in and up.

© Harcourt

First Aid

For Dental Emergencies

Dental emergencies occur less often than other health emergencies, but it is wise to know how to handle them

Broken Tooth

- Rinse your mouth with warm water. Wrap a cloth around a cold pack, and place it on the injured area. Save any parts of the broken tooth. Call your dentist immediately.

Bitten Tongue or Lip

- Apply direct pressure to the bleeding area with a cloth. Use a wrapped cold pack to stop swelling. If the bleeding doesn't stop within fifteen minutes, go to a hospital emergency room.

Knocked-Out Permanent Tooth

- Find the tooth, and clean it gently and carefully. Handle it by the top (crown), not the root. Put it back into the socket if you can. Hold it in place by biting on a piece of clean cloth. If the tooth cannot be put back in, place it in a cup with milk or water. See a dentist immediately because time is very important in saving the tooth.

Food or Objects Caught Between Teeth

- Use dental floss to gently take out the food or object. Never use anything sharp to remove what is stuck between your teeth. If it cannot be removed, call your dentist.

Remember that many dental injuries can be prevented if you

- wear a mouth guard while playing sports.
- wear a safety belt while riding in a car.
- inspect your home and get rid of hazards that might cause falls and injuries.
- see your dentist regularly for preventive care.

Health and Safety Handbook

For Insect Bites and Stings

- Always tell an adult about bites and stings.

- Scrape out the stinger with your fingernail.

- Wash the area with soap and water.

- A wrapped ice cube or cold pack will usually take away the pain from insect bites. A paste made from baking soda and water also helps.

- If the bite or sting is more serious and is on an arm or leg, keep the leg or arm dangling down. Apply a cold, wet cloth. Get help immediately!

millimeters

- If you find a tick on your skin, remove it. Protect your fingers with a tissue or cloth to prevent contact with infectious tick fluids. If you must touch the tick with your bare hands, wash your hands right away.

- If the tick has already bitten you, ask an adult to remove it. Using tweezers, an adult should grab the tick as close to your skin as possible and pull the tick out in one steady motion. Do not use petroleum jelly or oil of any kind because it may cause the tick to struggle, releasing its infectious fluids. Thoroughly wash the area of the bite.

For Skin Rashes from Plants

Many poisonous plants have three leaves. Remember, "Leaves of three, let them be." If you touch a poisonous plant, wash the area and your hands. Change clothes, and wash the ones the plant touched. If a rash develops, follow these tips.

- Apply calamine lotion or a paste of baking soda and water. Try not to scratch. Tell an adult.

- If you get blisters, do not pop them. If they burst, keep the area clean and dry. Cover the area with a bandage.

- If your rash does not go away in two weeks or if the rash is on your face or in your eyes, see your doctor.

Alcohol, Tobacco, and Other Drugs
A Drug-Free School

Schools help their students refuse to use alcohol, tobacco, and other drugs. Many schools make rules and sponsor activities to encourage people to say *no* to drugs.

DRUG-FREE SCHOOL ZONE

MINIMUM 3 YEARS IN PRISON TO SELL, PURCHASE, MANUFACTURE, DELIVER OR POSSESS WITH INTENT TO SELL AN ILLEGAL DRUG WITHIN 1,000 FEET OF A SCHOOL
STATE STATUTE 893

School Rules

Your school probably has rules about drugs. Many schools decide to be drug-free zones. They often have strict penalties for anyone found with drugs. For example, anyone found with drugs may be expelled or suspended. Learn your school's rules regarding use of drugs.

Positive Peer Pressure

Peer pressure can be bad or good. When people the same age encourage each other to make healthful choices, they are using *positive peer pressure*. In a school, students may make posters or hold rallies to encourage other students to choose not to use drugs.

© Harcourt

Alcohol, Tobacco, and Other Drugs

What to Do When Others Use Drugs

You should make a commitment not to use alcohol, tobacco, or other drugs. But you may be around other students or adults who make unhealthful choices. Here is what you can do.

Know the Signs

If someone has a problem with drugs, he or she often acts differently. The person may be sad or angry all the time, skip school or work, or forget important events.

Talk to a Trusted Adult

If you are worried about someone's drug use, don't keep it a secret. Talk to a trusted adult. Ask the adult for help. You can also get support from adults to resist pressure to use drugs.

Be Supportive

If a person has decided to stop using drugs, help him or her stop. Suggest healthful activities you can do together. Tell the person you're happy that he or she has stopped using drugs.

Stay Healthy

If you have a choice, leave any place where drugs are being used. If you cannot leave, stay as far away from the drugs as possible.

Where to Get Help

- Hospitals
- Alateen
- Alcoholics Anonymous
- Narcotics Anonymous
- Al-Anon
- Drug treatment centers

© Harcourt

Health and Safety
Backpack Safety

Carrying a backpack that is too heavy can injure your back. Carrying one incorrectly also can hurt you.

Safe Use

- Choose a backpack with wide, padded shoulder straps and a padded back.

- Lighten your load. Leave unnecessary items at home.

- Pack heavier items so that they will be closest to your back.

- Always use both shoulder straps to carry the backpack.

- Never wear a backpack while riding a bicycle. The weight makes it harder to stay balanced. Use the bicycle's basket or saddlebags instead.

▲ This is the right way to wear a backpack.

▲ This is the wrong way to carry a backpack

Safe Weight

A full backpack should weigh no more than 10 to 15 percent of your body weight. Less is better. To find 10 percent, divide your body weight by 10. Here are some examples:

Your Weight (pounds)	Maximum Backpack Weight (pounds)
70	7
80	8
90	9

Health and Safety Handbook

Health and Safety

Bike Safety Check

A safe bike should be the right size for you.

- You should be able to rest your heel on the pedal when you sit on your bike with the pedal in the lowest position.

- When you are standing astride your bike with both feet flat on the ground, your body should be 2 inches above the bar that goes from the handlebar to the seat.

A bike should have all the safety equipment shown below. Does *your* bike pass the test?

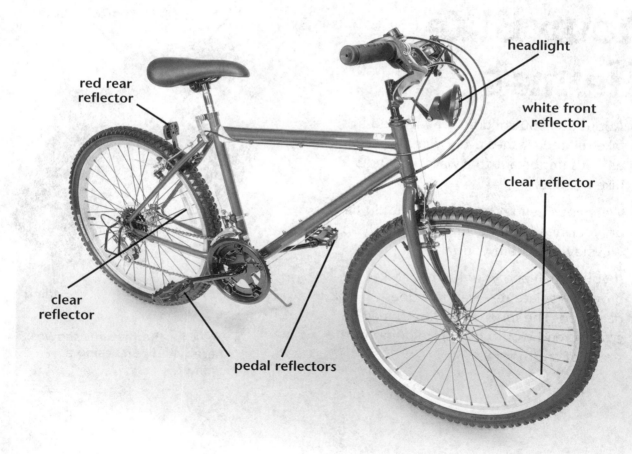

red rear reflector

headlight

white front reflector

clear reflector

clear reflector

pedal reflectors

Safety While Riding

Here are some tips for safe bicycle riding.

- Always wear your bike helmet, even for short distances.

- Check your bike every time you ride it. Is it in safe working condition?

- Ride in single file in the same direction as traffic. Never weave in and out of parked cars.

- Before you enter a street, **Stop. Look** left, right, and then left again. **Listen** for any traffic. **Think** before you go.

- Walk your bike across an intersection. **Look** left, right, and then left again. Wait for traffic to pass.

- Obey all traffic signs and signals.

- Do not ride your bike at night without an adult. Be sure to wear light-colored clothing, have reflectors, and use front and rear lights for night riding.

Your Bike Helmet

- About 500,000 children are involved in bike-related crashes every year. That's why it's important to always wear your bike helmet.

- Wear your helmet properly. It should lie flat on your head and be strapped snugly so it will stay in place if you fall.

- If you do fall and your helmet strikes the ground, replace it—even if it doesn't look damaged. The inner foam lining may be crushed and would not protect you in the event of another fall.

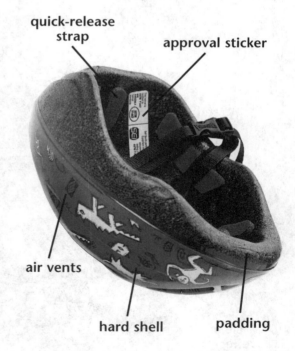

quick-release strap

approval sticker

air vents

hard shell

padding

▲ Look for the features shown here when purchasing a helmet.

© Harcourt

Health and Safety

Summer and Backyard Safety

Use this list to check for hazards before playing in your own or a friend's backyard.

Poison Plants such as poison ivy, poinsettias, certain mushrooms, and oleander are just some of the plants that are poisonous. Use caution around yard chemicals, such as fertilizers, pesticides, pool chemicals, and pet products.

Water Do not leave small children unattended near swimming pools, kiddie pools, and large basins. Use a life jacket when boating. Wear boat shoes around wet and slippery decks.

Strangling Hazards Use caution around fences, decks, and stairway railings. Clothes-lines and rope can also be hazardous if a small child gets caught in them. Always use care when playing on or around swings.

Insects and Other Animals Remember that ticks, mosquitoes, bees, or other flying insects can cause diseases or bites that can be fatal. Strange dogs wandering into your backyard may be dangerous and should be avoided.

Fire Be careful around barbecue grills, lighter fluid, and bonfires. Fires can get out of hand very quickly, and accidents can happen before anyone realizes what is happening.

Cutting Tools and Power Tools Treat lawn mowers and all power tools with respect. Never leave them unattended where a child might turn them on.

Falling Remember to use good sense and good manners around climbing bars, ladders, and tree houses. Pushing or shoving a person can cause cuts, broken bones, and knocked-out teeth.

Sun Remember to use sunscreen, wear a hat, and drink plenty of liquids when out in the sun. Sunburn or heatstroke can put a quick or painful end to a fun day.

Thunderstorm Safety

Thunderstorms are severe storms. Lightning can injure or kill people, cause fires, and damage property. Here are thunderstorm safety tips.

- **If you are inside**, **stay there.** The safest place to be is inside a building.

- **If you are outside**, **try to take shelter.** If possible, get into a closed car or truck. If you can't take shelter, get into a ditch or another low area.

- **If you are outside**, **stay away from tall objects.** Don't stand in an open field, on a beach, on a hilltop, or near a lone tree. Find a low place and crouch down, with only your feet touching the ground.

- **Stay away from water.** Lightning is attracted to water, and water conducts electricity.

- **Listen for weather bulletins.** Storms that produce lightning may also produce tornadoes. Be ready to take shelter in a basement or in a hallway or other room without windows.

Earthquake Safety

An earthquake is a strong shaking of the ground. The tips below, many for adults, can help you and your family stay safe.

Before an Earthquake	During an Earthquake	After an Earthquake
• Bolt tall, heavy furniture, such as bookcases, to the wall. Store the heaviest items on the lowest shelves.	• If you are outdoors, stay there. Move away from buildings and electric wires.	• Continue to watch for falling objects as aftershocks shake the area.
• To prevent fires, bolt down gas appliances and use flexible hose and connections for both gas and water lines.	• If you are indoors, stay under heavy furniture or in a doorway. Stay away from glass doors and windows and heavy objects that might fall.	• Have the building checked for hidden structural problems.
• Firmly anchor overhead light fixtures to the ceiling to keep them from falling.	• If you are in a car, go to an open area away from buildings and overpasses.	• Check for broken gas, electric, and water lines. If you smell gas, shut off the gas main and leave the area. Report the leak.

© Harcourt

Blizzard Safety

A blizzard is a dangerous snowstorm with strong winds and heavy snowfall. It may last for 12 to 36 hours, with snowfall greater than 6 inches in 24 hours and winds gusting higher than 35 miles per hour. Visibility may be less than $\frac{1}{4}$ mile. The following tips can help you and your family stay safe during a blizzard.

Your home should have

- a working flashlight with extra batteries.
- a battery-powered NOAA weather radio, radio, or TV.
- extra food and water, plus medicines and baby items if needed.
- first-aid supplies.
- heating fuel such as propane, kerosene, or fuel oil.
- an emergency heating source.
- a smoke detector and a fire extinguisher.

If traveling by car or truck, your family should

- keep the gas tank nearly full. The vehicle should be fully checked and properly prepared for winter use.
- always let a friend or relative know the family's travel plans.
- keep a blizzard survival kit in the vehicle. It should contain blankets; a flashlight with extra batteries; a can and waterproof matches to melt snow for drinking; and high-calorie, nonperishable food.
- remain in the vehicle in a blizzard, and tie something bright to the antenna. Run the motor for short times for heat. Use the inside light only while running the motor.

Health and Safety

Evaluating Health Websites

Many people find health facts on the Web. The Web is a valuable information resource. However, it's important to remember that almost anyone can put information on the Web. You need to learn how to tell good, reliable websites from bad, unreliable ones. Here are some questions to think about when you are looking at health websites.

Who controls the website?

A site can be biased, or slanted, toward one viewpoint. Look for sources that you know. Sites run by a university (.edu) or by the government (.gov) are usually more reliable. A site run by one person whom you've never heard of is probably less reliable.

Who is saying it?

Information from doctors, nurses, and health professionals is usually reliable. Look for the initials of a college degree after the writer's name—*M.D., R.N., Ph.D., Pharm.D.,* and so on. Reputable newspaper and magazine sites usually check their facts with a health professional, so, they're usually reliable as well.

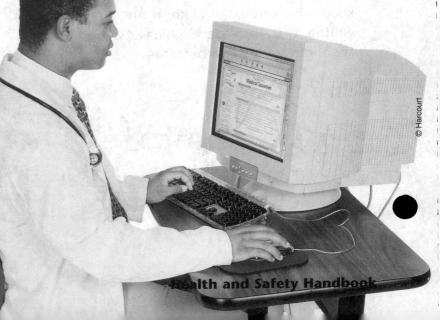

© Harcourt

Does the site look good?

Frequent spelling or grammar mistakes and poor design are warning signs. If the site didn't take time to fix simple mistakes, perhaps it didn't take the time to check the facts, either.

Are they selling something?

Sites that are trying to sell a product may not be reliable. Often, they tell you only what makes their products or services look good. Nonprofit sites are usually more reliable.

What is the evidence?

Personal stories sound convincing. However, they are not as reliable as scientifically tested information. Look for sites with evidence from science research.

Does everyone agree?

Always try to check more than one source. If several sites agree on the facts, they are probably reliable.

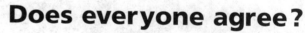

Health and Safety

Good Posture at the Computer

Good posture is very important when using the computer. To help prevent eyestrain, muscle fatigue, and injuries, follow the posture tips shown below. Remember to grasp your mouse lightly, keep your back straight, avoid facing your monitor toward a window, and take frequent breaks for stretching.

top of screen at or just below eye level

shoulders in line with ears and hips

neck and shoulders relaxed

arms at sides, bent as shown

wrists straight

feet flat on floor

© Harcourt

Safety on the Internet

The Internet is a remarkable tool. You can use it for fun, education, research, and more. However, like anything else, it has some downsides. Some people compare the Internet to a city—not all the people there are people you want to meet, and not all the places you can go are places you want to be. On the Internet, as in a real city, you have to use common sense and follow safety guidelines to protect yourself. Below are some easy rules you can follow to stay safe online.

Rules for Online Safety

- Talk with an adult family member to set up rules for going online. Decide when you can go online, how long you can be online, and what kinds of places you can visit. Do not break the rules you agree to follow.

- Don't give out personal information such as your name, address, and telephone number or information about your family. Don't give the name or location of your school.

- If you find anything online that makes you uncomfortable, tell an adult family member right away.

- Never agree to meet with anyone in person. If you want to get together with someone you have met online, check with an adult family member first. If a meeting is approved, arrange to meet in a public place, and bring an adult with you.

- Don't send your picture or anything else to a person you meet online without first checking with an adult.

- Don't respond to any messages that are mean or make you uncomfortable. If you receive a message like that, tell an adult right away.

Health and Safety
Family Emergency Plan

By having a plan, your family can protect itself during an emergency. To make an emergency plan, your family needs to gather information, make some choices, and practice parts of the plan.

Know What Could Happen

Learn the possible emergencies that might happen in your area. Fires and storms can happen almost anywhere. You may also be at risk for earthquakes or floods. List the possible emergencies.

Have Two Meeting Places

Pick two places to meet, one near your home and one farther away. The first place should be only far enough away to be safe in case of a fire. For example, you could meet at the corner of your block. The second place could be the main door to your school, a relative's house, or where a family member works.

Know Your Family Contact

Choose someone who lives far away to be a contact person. This person will help your family stay in touch. If a family member becomes lost during an emergency, he or she can call the contact person. Each family member should memorize the full name, address, and telephone number of the contact.

Out-of-State Contact
Ms. Jane Doe
43212 Janeway Blvd.
Big City, IL 12345
(123) 555-1234

© Harcourt

Practice Evacuating

During a fire, you need to evacuate, or get out of, your home right away. Look at your list of possible emergencies. Use it to help you plan how to evacuate each room of your home. Practice evacuating at least twice a year.

▼ This woman is showing her daughter how to turn off the main water valve at their home.

▲ outdoor water shut-off valve

Learn How to Turn Off Utilities

Water, electricity, and gas are *utilities*. An emergency may damage utility pipes or wires and make them dangerous. This can damage or even destroy a home. With an adult's help, learn when and how to turn off utilities. If tools are needed to turn off a utility, those tools should be stored close by. **CAUTION:** If you turn off the gas, a professional must turn it back on.

Make an Emergency Supply Kit

After an emergency, your family may need food, blankets, clean water to drink, and first-aid supplies. The American Red Cross or other emergency organizations can give your family a checklist for making an emergency supply kit.

1. STOP

Fire Safety

Fires cause more deaths than any other type of disaster. But a fire doesn't have to be deadly if you and your family prepare your home and follow some basic safety rules.

- Install smoke detectors outside sleeping areas and on any additional floors of your home. Be sure to test the smoke detectors once a month and change the batteries in each detector twice a year.

- Keep a fire extinguisher on each floor of your home. Check monthly to make sure each is properly charged.

- Make a family emergency plan. See page 118 for help. Ideally, there should be two routes out of each room. Sleeping areas are most important, because most fires happen at night. Plan to use stairs only; elevators can be dangerous in a fire.

- Designate one person to call the fire department or 911 from a neighbor's home.

- Practice crawling low to avoid smoke. If your clothes catch fire, follow the three steps shown.

2. DROP

3. ROLL

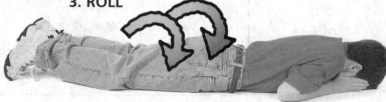

© Harcourt

Health and Safety
Caring for Your Skin

- Your skin is a complicated organ that protects you from diseases and helps keep your body from drying out.

- A daily bath or shower helps remove dirt, germs, dead skin cells, and excess oil from your skin.

- Because of all the changes that occur during puberty, it is very important to practice good hygiene to control body odor.

▲ **Using products such as these will keep your skin clean and healthy.**

▲ **Using sunscreen even on cloudy days will protect your skin from the sun's harmful rays.**

- The sun can be more damaging for your skin than dirt and germs. Too much sun can make your skin become wrinkled, tough, and leathery. It can also cause skin cancer, which can lead to death.

- Covering up with clothing and wearing a hat give you good protection from the sun. Protect uncovered skin with sunscreen, even on cloudy days.

Health and Safety
Safety near Water

Water can be very dangerous—a person can drown in five minutes or less. The best way to be safer near water is to learn how to swim. You should also follow these rules:

- Never swim without a lifeguard or a responsible adult present.

- If you can't swim, stay in shallow water. Don't rely on an inflatable raft.

- Know the rules for the beach or pool, and obey them. Don't run or play roughly near water.

- Do not dive in head-first until you know the water is deep enough. Jump in feet-first the first time.

- Watch the weather. Get out of the water at once if you see lightning or hear thunder.

- Protect your skin with sunscreen and your eyes with sunglasses.

- Wear a Coast Guard-approved life jacket anytime you are in a boat.

- Know what to do in an emergency.

© Harcourt

While you are caring for children, you should

- never leave a baby alone on a changing table, sofa, or bed.
- never leave a child alone, even for a short time.
- check children often when they are sleeping.
- never leave a child alone near a pool or in the bathtub.
- never let a child play with a plastic bag.
- keep dangerous items out of a child's reach.
- know where all the doors are, and keep them locked. Do not let anyone in without permission from the adults.
- take a message if the phone rings. Do not tell the caller that you are the babysitter or that the adults are out.
- call the adults if there is an injury or illness. If you can't reach them, call the emergency numbers on the list.

▲ Never leave children playing alone.

▲ Never leave a child to eat alone.

◄ Never leave children alone near a pool or in the bathtub.

© Harcourt

Health and Safety

When Home Alone

Everyone stays home alone sometimes. When you stay home alone, it's important to know how to take care of yourself. Here are some easy rules to follow that will help keep you safe when you are home by yourself.

Do These Things

- Lock all the doors and windows. Be sure you know how to lock and unlock all the locks.

- If someone who is nasty or mean calls, say nothing and hang up immediately. Tell an adult about the call when he or she gets home. Your parents may not want you to answer the phone at all.

- If you have an emergency, call 911. Be prepared to describe the problem and to give your full name, address, and telephone number. Follow all instructions given to you. Do not hang up the phone until you are told to do so.

- If you see anyone hanging around outside your home, call a neighbor or the police.

- If you see or smell smoke, go outside right away. If you live in an apartment, do not take the elevator. Go to a neighbor's house, and call 911 immediately.

- Entertain yourself. Time will pass more quickly if you are not bored. Work on a hobby, read a book or magazine, do your homework, or clean your room. Before you know it, an adult will be home.

Do Not Do These Things

- Do NOT use the stove, microwave, or oven unless an adult family member has given you permission and you know how to use these appliances.

- Do NOT open the door to anyone you don't know or to anyone who is not supposed to be in your home.

- Do NOT talk to strangers on the telephone. Do not tell anyone that you are home alone. If the call is for an adult family member, say that he or she can't come to the phone right now and take a message.

- Do NOT have friends over unless an adult family member has given you permission to do so.

© Harcourt

▶ A caller ID display can help you decide whether to answer the phone.

Activity Book Answer Key • Chapter 1

A Growing and Changing Body

Quick Study
Pages 1–2

Lesson 1

Summary: cell, tissues, organs, system
Lesson Details: Cells ➡ Tissues ➡ Organs ➡ Transport systems; Respiratory system, Digestive system, Excretory system

Lesson 2

Summary: joint, ligaments, tendons, Neurons
Lesson Details: Possible answer: Nerves send messages directly to the spinal cord, which tells muscles to react. The message does not go through the brain.

Lesson 3

Summary: heredity, environment, hormones
Lesson Details: Possible answers: Bones grow by making new cells, so they need materials from food to make the new cells. Physical activity makes muscles grow thicker and stronger. Muscles use nutrients from food to repair themselves.

Lesson 4

Summary: prenatal, growth spurt
Lesson Details:
1. c and d
2. b and f
3. a and e

Lesson 5

Summary: concrete thinking, abstract thinking
Lesson Details: 3, 2, 4, 1

Reading Skill
Page 3

Heart ➡ Lungs ➡ Heart ➡ Arteries ➡ Capillaries ➡ Veins

Problem Solving
Page 4

A. Possible answer: Alicia did steps 1 and 2 just right. Alicia used "I" messages to tell Maria how she felt, and she listened to Maria while she explained why she didn't want to lend her shirt. However, Alicia forgot to negotiate and find a way for both of them to win. Alicia could have offered to lend Maria something of hers or to replace Maria's shirt if it got damaged.

B. Possible answer: Antonio could tell Greg to talk to his brother and tell him how he feels. Greg should listen to his brother to understand why he doesn't do his chores anymore. Perhaps he has less time now or is tired. Then Greg could offer to help his brother with his chores if he will let him use his CD player, pay Greg for doing the chores, or treat him to a movie now and then. Greg and his brother should be able to find something that they can both feel good about.

Vocabulary Reinforcement
Page 5

A. cell, tissue, alveoli, nephrons, joint
B. **Across**
   1. heredity
   3. hygiene
   5. hormones
   6. body image
   7. prenatal
   8. concrete
   9. growth spurt
   10. tendons
   Down
   2. environment
   4. reflex action
   7. puberty

Activity Book Answer Key • Chapter 2

Being a Wise Health Consumer

Quick Study
Pages 6–7

Lesson 1

Summary: SPF, ultraviolet rays, hair follicle, oil glands

Lesson Details:
- Acne develops when pores become clogged with dirt and oil.
- Acne causes pimples.
- Keeping pores open by washing regularly may help control pimples.

Lesson 2

Summary: plaque, gingivitis, orthodontia

Lesson Details:
- Acids form when bacteria in plaque break down sugars in foods.
- These acids can form holes called cavities in teeth.

Lesson 3

Summary: nearsighted, farsighted, astigmatism, decibels

Lesson Details:
1. True
2. False
3. True

Lesson 4

Summary: health consumer, ingredients

Lesson Details:
1. products
2. information
3. myths

Reading Skill
Page 8

What I read: Students should summarize important details from the article.

What I know about how quickly I get a sunburn: Students should indicate how quickly they burn.

Conclusion: Answers will vary, but standard would be 450 minutes.

Problem Solving
Page 9

A. Possible answer: Denzel can explain that germs can be passed from one person to another by unwashed hands. He can make sure there are soap, nail brushes, and towels and a proper place for everyone to wash up.

B. Possible answer: First, she should explain that the most important thing the product must do is protect the girls' skin from ultraviolet rays. Marta can suggest that they compare prices and ingredients of three brands. Then they can add other criteria to use as they make comparisons.

Vocabulary Reinforcement
Page 10

A. **Across**
   1. hair follicle
   3. gingivitis
   5. plaque
   6. orthodontia
   9. ultraviolet

   Down
   1. health consumer
   2. oil gland
   4. SPF
   7. far
   8. near

B. Check students' sentences for content.

Learning About Disease

Quick Study
Pages 31–32

Lesson 1

Summary: communicable disease, noncommunicable disease

Lesson Details: Possible answer: Give the person help when he or she needs it. Treat him or her as you would treat other people. [these answers can be in any order]

Lesson 2

Summary: symptoms, pathogens, infection, abstinence

Lesson Details: Possible answers:

Viruses   colds, chicken pox, HIV
Bacteria   strep throat, TB, Lyme disease
Fungi   athlete's foot, ringworm
Protozoa   giardiasis, amebic dysentery

Lesson 3

Summary: Antibodies, immunity, vaccine, antibiotic, resistance

Lesson Details: Answers will vary. Possible answers: *Tears* kill and wash away pathogens that enter your eyes. *Cilia* along breathing passages keep pathogens out of your lungs. Chemicals in *saliva* kill pathogens that enter your mouth. *Ear wax* traps pathogens that enter your ears. *Mucus* traps pathogens in your nose and keeps them from getting into your respiratory system. *Stomach acid* kills most pathogens in your digestive system. The *skin's* outer layers block pathogens.

Lesson 4

Summary: immunization

Lesson Details: Possible answers: blood pressure check, listen to heart and lungs

Lesson 5

Summary: chronic, acute, Insulin, seizure

Lesson Details:

Not using sunscreen   skin cancer
Using smokeless tobacco   mouth cancer
Overeating junk foods   heart disease

Lesson 6

Summary: Aerobic exercise

Lesson Details: Possible answers:
Eat a healthful diet. Avoid tobacco products. Get plenty of exercise.

Reading Skill
Page 33

Main Idea: Pathogens cause communicable diseases.

Details: Pathogens are bacteria, viruses, fungi, protozoa. Some bacterial infections can be treated with antibiotics. Some viral diseases can be prevented by vaccines.

Summary: Pathogens cause communicable diseases. Some of these diseases can be treated with antibiotics or prevented with vaccines.

Problem Solving
Page 34

A. Possible answer: Keisha's stress is caused by doing too much. She should talk to a parent or another trusted adult about reducing her activities or rearranging her schedule. She should think positively about doing well at the activities she chooses to continue.

B. Possible answer: Nate's stress is making him feel sick to his stomach. He should talk to his parents or his art teacher and share his worries about his drawings. He should think about the benefits of competing.

Vocabulary Reinforcement
Page 35

1. acute
2. noncommunicable disease
3. bacteria
4. resistance
5. symptoms
6. antibodies
7. immunity
8. Seizures
9. insulin
10. fungi

© Harcourt

Activity Book Answer Key • Chapter 8

Legal and Illegal Drugs

Quick Study
Pages 36–37

Lesson 1

Summary: drug; medicines; prescription medicines

Lesson Details: Both medicines may help you feel better, if used properly. Prescription medicines must be ordered by a doctor. OTC medicines can be bought without a doctor's order. Prescription medicines have directions for one person. OTC medicines have directions for everyone.

Lesson 2

Summary: dosage, self-medicating, medicine abuse

Lesson Details:

depression	fatigue	violent behavior
hair loss	irritability	severe acne

Lesson 3

Summary: Illegal drugs, overdose, withdrawal

Lesson Details:

Speeds up body functions, causes people to become violent

Changes brain functions, decreases coordination, damages lungs

Cause headaches, confusion, memory loss, nose-bleeds, damage to brain, kidneys, and liver

Lesson 4

Summary: refuse

Lesson Details: Possible answers: walk away, politely but firmly say *no*, explain that your parents trust you to refuse, say *no* and tell why not

Lesson 5

Summary: behavior, adult

Lesson Details: Answers may vary; possible answers given.

1. sudden weight loss   3. often missing school
2. asking to borrow money

Reading Skill
Page 38

Effect:

• The medicine helps the person recover from the infection.

• The person may suffer from side effects from mixing medicines or an overdose from taking too much medicine.

• The person feels that he or she must have more and more of the medicine. Addiction can cause illness or death.

Problem Solving
Page 39

A. Possible answer: Jerry and Mike could say *no* to the boys and tell them that the reason they refuse to smoke marijuana is that it can cause short-term memory loss, slow reaction time, and harm the immune system. It can also cause unpleasant side effects, is illegal, and is against their families' rules.

B. Possible answer: Lakisha could say *no* to Kendra's idea and suggest that they get started studying. In the future, Lakisha could choose to spend her time with people who don't make harmful decisions.

Vocabulary Reinforcement
Page 40

A. 1. d   5. c
       2. e   6. g
       3. b   7. a
       4. h   8. f

B. Check students' sentences.

© Harcourt

Teaching Resources Answer Key • Communicable Diseases

Mad Cow Disease
Pages 121–122

1. Possible answer: Mad Cow disease is a serious illness. There is no cure. You can get it by eating infected meat.
2. a. protein; b. United Kingdom; c. few
3. Possible answers: infected meat is not sold to the public; infected people do not donate blood or organs; infected cows are removed from herds; doctors and nurses follow safety guidelines.

West Nile Virus
Pages 123–124

1. Possible details: stay inside near sunrise and sunset; wear long-sleeve shirts, long pants, and use insect spray with DEET; repair screens; clean up standing water
2. Some have no symptoms; others have fever, chills, upset stomach, and sometimes a rash; a few have a high fever, problems seeing, and numbness.
3. bird; glands; animal; 3 to 14
4. The virus was first discovered in west Uganda near the Nile River.

Lyme Disease
Pages 125–126

1. Wear light colored clothing including a shirt with long sleeves, long pants, and a hat. Ask an adult to remove the tick with tweezers. Check carefully for ticks on your body; wash clothes in hot water.
2. Possible answer: bull's-eye rash, fever, chills, headache, joint and muscle pain
3. did not cover up — cover up with long sleeves, long pants, and a hat; left the path — stay in center of the trail; did not check for ticks — check for ticks before going inside

Staphylococcus Infection
Pages 127–128

1. skin, blood, lungs
2. by touching an infected area, then touching a cut on your body
3. Julie dries with a towel. Tom gets a staph infection.
4. Possible answer: Keep cuts and scrapes covered with a bandage. Wash cuts with soap and water. Do not share towels.